The Benefits to Taxpayers from Increases in Students' Educational Attainment

Stephen J. Carroll, Emre Erkut

Supported by the The William and Flora Hewlett Foundation

 EDUCATION

The research in this report was produced within RAND Education, a unit of the RAND Corporation, with support from the William and Flora Hewlett Foundation.

Library of Congress Cataloging-in-Publication Data

Carroll, Stephen J., 1940–
 The benefits to taxpayers from increases in students' educational attainment / Stephen J. Carroll, Emre Erkut.
  p. cm.
 Includes bibliographical references.
 ISBN 978-0-8330-4742-7 (pbk. : alk. paper)
 1. Public schools—United States—Finance. 2. Education—United States—Finance. 3. Income tax—United States. I. Erkut, Emre. II. Title.

LB2825.C315 2009
379.1'10973—dc22

2009024776

The RAND Corporation is a nonprofit research organization providing objective analysis and effective solutions that address the challenges facing the public and private sectors around the world. RAND's publications do not necessarily reflect the opinions of its research clients and sponsors.

RAND® is a registered trademark.

© Copyright 2009 RAND Corporation

Permission is given to duplicate this document for personal use only, as long as it is unaltered and complete. Copies may not be duplicated for commercial purposes. Unauthorized posting of RAND documents to a non-RAND Web site is prohibited. RAND documents are protected under copyright law. For information on reprint and linking permissions, please visit the RAND permissions page (http://www.rand.org/publications/permissions.html).

Published 2009 by the RAND Corporation
1776 Main Street, P.O. Box 2138, Santa Monica, CA 90407-2138
1200 South Hayes Street, Arlington, VA 22202-5050
4570 Fifth Avenue, Suite 600, Pittsburgh, PA 15213-2665
RAND URL: http://www.rand.org/
To order RAND documents or to obtain additional information, contact
Distribution Services: Telephone: (310) 451-7002;
Fax: (310) 451-6915; Email: order@rand.org

Preface

Meeting the educational demands of the future will be expensive; however, in most states, public schools from kindergarten through the university level already experience budgetary challenges. Policymakers face a fundamental challenge—motivating taxpayers to provide the funds needed to meet mounting education needs.

This report examines the financial benefits that taxpayers realize when students' educational attainment is increased. We find that the benefits to taxpayers from increases in students' educational attainment are very high. Regardless of a student's gender or race/ethnicity, raising his or her level of education leads, on average, to substantially increased payments into, and reduced demands on, the public budget. We consider the cost of providing additional education to students, although we do not explore the question of what it would cost to motivate students to stay longer in school. Our analysis indicates that taxpayers accrue benefits from programs and policies that succeed in raising students' education levels, and those benefits are entirely separate from the benefits that the students themselves gain through increased education. Accordingly, taxpayers, including those who do not have children in school, have a stake in developing programs and policies that effectively and efficiently increase education levels.

This report's findings should be of interest to a broad range of policymakers, researchers, administrators, teachers, and parents.

This research was conducted within RAND Education, a division of the RAND Corporation, with support from the William and Flora Hewlett Foundation.

Contents

Preface iii
Figures ix
Tables xi
Summary xiii
Acknowledgments xxi
Abbreviations xxiii

CHAPTER ONE
Introduction 1
The Problem 1
Research Objective 2
   The Costs of Providing Education Versus the Overall Costs of Increasing
      Educational Attainment 2
Research Questions 3
Illustrative Examples 5
Previous Research 7
Definition of Terms 9
Organization of the Report 10

CHAPTER TWO
Analytic Approach 13
Independent Variables 13
Education and Earnings 14
Tax Payments 18
   Federal Income Taxes 18
   State and Local Taxes 19
   Payroll Taxes 19
Social Program Participation and Costs 19
Incarceration Costs 21
Estimating the Effects of Increased Education 22
Transformations 24

Critical Assumptions 25
Putting the Results in Perspective. 27

CHAPTER THREE
Payments for Taxes and Social Programs 29
Taxation Mechanisms 29
Educational Attainment and Earnings 31
Federal and State Tax Rates. 32
 Federal Income Tax Rates 32
 Payroll Tax Rates. 33
 Average State Tax Rates 34
The Effects of Increased Educational Attainment on Tax Payments. 34
Related Studies 36
The Effects of Multilevel Increases in Educational Attainment on Tax Payments 37
Sensitivity Analysis. 37
Summary 39

CHAPTER FOUR
Spending on Social Support Programs 41
Background 41
Analytic Approach 42
Effects of Educational Attainment on the Costs of Welfare Programs 44
Effects of Educational Attainment on the Costs of Housing Subsidies 46
Effects of Educational Attainment on the Costs of Food Stamps. 47
Effects of Educational Attainment on Supplemental Security Income Spending. 49
Effects of Educational Attainment on Medicaid Spending 50
Effects of Educational Attainment on Medicare Spending 52
Effects of Educational Attainment on the Costs of Unemployment Insurance 53
Effects of Educational Attainment on Social Security Spending. 55
Effects of Educational Attainment on Spending on Social Programs 56
Sensitivity Analysis. 58
Summary 60

CHAPTER FIVE
Educational Attainment and Spending on the Corrections System 61
Analytic Approach 62
The Effect of Educational Attainment on Crime Rates 63
Effects of Educational Attainment on Incarceration Costs 65
Sensitivity Analysis. 67
Summary 68

CHAPTER SIX
The Costs of Providing Additional Education 69

CHAPTER SEVEN
Educational Attainment and Public Revenues and Costs 73
Effects of Increases in Education on the Public Budget 73
    Tax Payments 73
    Spending on Social Support and Insurance Programs 74
    Incarceration Costs 74
    Costs of Increased Education 75
Net Benefits from Increased Educational Attainment 75
The Effects of Increased Educational Attainment: An Example 80
Sensitivity Analysis 82
Putting the Estimates in Perspective 84
Summary 85

APPENDIXES
A. Data and Sources 87
B. Estimating Tax Payments 91
C. Social Program Participation and Costs 95
D. Incarceration Cost Estimations 111

References 113

Figures

3.1.	Present Value of Lifetime Increases in Tax Payments Resulting from Increased Education, U.S.-Born Men	35
3.2.	Present Value of Lifetime Increases in Tax Payments Resulting from Increased Educational Attainment, U.S.-Born Women	36
4.1.	Expected Annual Welfare Program Spending for a U.S.-Born Hispanic Woman	45
4.2.	Expected Annual Public Housing Subsidies for a U.S.-Born Hispanic Woman	47
4.3.	Expected Annual Food Stamp Benefits for a U.S.-Born Hispanic Woman	48
4.4.	Expected Annual Supplemental Security Income for a U.S.-Born Hispanic Woman	50
4.5.	Expected Annual Medicaid Benefits for a U.S.-Born Hispanic Woman	51
4.6.	Expected Annual Medicare Benefits for a U.S.-Born Hispanic Woman	53
4.7.	Expected Annual Unemployment Compensation for a U.S.-Born Hispanic Woman	54
4.8.	Expected Annual Social Security Benefits for a U.S.-Born Hispanic Woman	56
4.9.	2002 Value of Lifetime Decrease in Social Program Spending Resulting from Increased Education for U.S.-Born Men	57
4.10.	2002 Value of Lifetime Decrease in Social Program Spending Resulting from Increased Education for U.S.-Born Women	58
5.1.	2002 Value of Lifetime Decrease in Incarceration Spending Resulting from Increased Education for U.S.-Born Men	66
5.2.	2002 Value of Lifetime Decrease in Incarceration Spending Resulting from Increased Education for U.S.-Born Women	67
7.1.	Benefits and Costs of Raising the Education of a U.S.-Born Hispanic Woman from Less Than High School Graduate to College Graduate	81

Tables

2.1.	Ratio of Median Usual Weekly Earnings of Full-time Wage and Salary Workers 25 Years and Over, by Educational Attainment	16
2.2.	Percentage of Persons Age 25 to 64 Who Are Employed, by Race/Ethnicity, Gender, and Education Level, 1992–2007	17
3.1a.	Average 2002 Individual Annual Earnings, by Ethnicity and Education Level	32
3.1b.	Average 2002 Family Annual Income, by Ethnicity and Education Level	32
3.2.	Average Federal Income Tax Rates and Related Data, by Income	33
3.3.	Statutory 2002 Payroll Tax Rates and Medicare Tax Cap	33
3.4.	State and Local Tax Rates for 2002, U.S. Average	34
3.5.	Increased Tax Payments Associated with Increasing Educational Attainment from High School Dropout to College Graduate, U.S.-Born Men and Women	38
3.6.	Range of Percentage Reduction in Tax Payments If the Effect of Increased Education Is Reduced 25 Percent, U.S.-Born Men and Women	38
3.7.	Smallest Estimated Effect of Increased Education on Tax Payments If Effect of Increased Education Is Reduced 25 Percent, U.S.-Born Men and Women	39
4.1.	Medicare and Medicaid Benefit Estimates, 2002	44
4.2.	Range of Percentage Reduction in Social Program Spending If Effect of Increased Education Is Reduced 25 Percent, U.S.-Born Men and Women	59
4.3.	Smallest Estimated Effect of Increased Education on Reduction in Social Program Spending If Effect of Increased Education Is Reduced 25 Percent, U.S.-Born Men and Women	59
5.1.	Educational Attainment for Inmates and the General Population	61
5.2.	Total and Unit Costs of Incarceration, 2002	62
5.3.	Present Value of Reduced Spending on Incarceration Associated with Increasing Educational Attainment from High School Dropout to College Graduate for U.S.-Born Individuals	68
7.1.	Effects of Increasing Education from High School Dropout to High School Graduate on Public Revenues and Costs for a U.S.-Born White Male	76

7.2.	Benefits to Taxpayers from Increasing Educational Attainment from Less Than High School to High School Graduate, U.S.-Born Men and Women	77
7.3.	Benefits to Taxpayers from Increasing Educational Attainment from High School Graduate to Some College, U.S.-Born Men and Women	78
7.4.	Benefits to Taxpayers from Increasing Educational Attainment from Some College to College Graduate, U.S.-Born Men and Women	79
7.5.	Benefits to Taxpayers from Increasing Educational Attainment from High School Dropout to College Graduate, U.S.-Born Men and Women	80
7.6.	Net Benefits from Increased Educational Attainment Among U.S.-Born Hispanics	82
7.7.	Range of Percentage Reduction in Net Benefits to Taxpayers If the Effect of Increased Education Is Reduced 25 Percent	82
7.8.	Smallest Estimated Effect of Increased Education on Net Benefits If Effect of Increased Education Is Reduced	83
B.1.	Estimated Two-Part Model of 2002 Payroll Tax Payments	92
B.2.	Estimates of 2002 Federal and State Tax Payments	94
C.1.	Estimated Two-Part Model of 2002 Welfare Income (Temporary Assistance to Needy Families, General Assistance, Other)	98
C.2.	Estimates of 2002 Subsidized Housing Participation	99
C.3.	Estimated Two-Part Model of 2002 Food Stamp Income	101
C.4a.	Estimated Two-Part Model of 2002 SSI Income	102
C.4b.	Estimated Two-Part Model of 2002 SSI Income	103
C.5.	Estimates of 2002 Medicaid Participation	105
C.6.	Estimates of 2002 Medicare Participation	106
C.7.	Estimated Two-Part Model of 2002 Unemployment Insurance Income	108
C.8a.	Estimated Two-Part Model of 2002 Social Security Income	109
C.8b.	Estimated Two-Part Model of 2002 Social Security Income	110

Summary

Policymakers in most states face a fundamental challenge—motivating taxpayers to provide the funds required to meet mounting educational needs. The level of education needed to succeed in labor markets and support economic growth is increasing rapidly. But, in most states, public schools from kindergarten through the university level already face budgetary limits, and meeting the demands of the future will be expensive. Taxpayers who do not have children in public school frequently question why they should contribute more to the support of educational institutions, or why those who stand to benefit the most—the students—should not pay more for their education.

In this study, we explore the financial benefits that taxpayers enjoy as a result of increases in students' education levels. We specifically address three research questions: How do increases in an individual's educational attainment affect

- tax revenues
- program expenditures and revenues for a range of social support and insurance programs
- spending for prisons and jails?

We then subtract the costs of providing additional education to a student from the estimated effects of an increase in his or her education level on public spending and revenues to estimate the net benefit to taxpayers resulting from the increase in an individual's education.

Our findings indicate that an increase in a student's educational attainment—say, completing high school rather than dropping out—results in substantial benefits to taxpayers over time. For example, if a U.S.-born, Hispanic man who would have dropped out of high school were to obtain a high school diploma instead, the discounted present value of the net benefits to taxpayers equals about $87,000 in 2002 dollars. The comparable result for a U.S.-born, Hispanic woman is almost as large, with net benefits equal to about $83,000 in 2002 dollars. The results for other racial and ethnic groups are similar.

Our analysis focuses on the net benefits to taxpayers from increases in educational attainment. However, this is not a cost-benefit analysis of specific programs, since we do not consider the costs of developing and operating programs and policies aimed at encouraging students to pursue higher education levels. Consequently, we do not know how the benefits from increases in education levels to taxpayers compare with the costs of policies and programs that induce students to increase their education. Our objective is to demonstrate that taxpayers gain certain benefits from programs and policies that result in greater educational attainment, even if the taxpayers do not have children in school, and that taxpayers should consequently consider these benefits in assessing the importance of developing and implementing programs and policies to increase education levels.

Analytic Approach

To address the research questions, we estimate the extent to which increased educational attainment will result in three types of benefits to taxpayers:

- increases in federal, state, and local tax revenues and increases in contributions to social support and insurance programs, such as Social Security and Medicare
- reductions in public expenditures on social support and insurance programs
- reductions in public expenditures on incarceration—the costs of operating state prisons and county and municipal jails.

By "increased educational attainment," we mean more time in school, rather than "better" education in the sense of the schools doing a better job. Similarly, when we talk about additional spending on education, we mean the spending required to serve individuals in school longer; we do not consider the costs of programs aimed at inducing students to remain in school longer.

We use a nationally representative sample of roughly 40,000 individuals covered in all months of 2002 by the Survey of Income and Program Participation (SIPP) to model the effects of education level (some high school, high school graduation, some college, and college graduation) on public revenues and expenditures, depending on an individual's age, gender, and race/ethnicity—African-American (black), Asian, Hispanic, Native American, or non-Hispanic white (white).

We estimate the effects of education level on federal, state, and local tax payments and payments into social support and insurance programs throughout the entire working life of an adult, using appropriate survival rates. We use federal data to estimate payments of federal taxes and contributions to social support and insurance programs, such as Social Security and Medicare. State and local tax schedules vary across the country, so we use U.S. national average state and local tax schedules to estimate state and local tax payments.

We examine the effects of education level on program spending for eight of the country's largest social support and insurance programs for which sufficient data on program participation and program spending are available. Different segments of the population participate at different rates in social support and insurance programs. Consequently, we conduct separate analyses for different groups distinguished by gender and race/ethnicity. Because the social programs we examine are all national programs, we use the national sample to model the effects of educational attainment on (1) the likelihood that a person will enroll in a social support or insurance program and (2) the amount of benefit that a person will receive from a social support program upon enrollment.

Incarceration rates and the costs of operating prisons and jails vary across the country. Because federal prisons house a small percentage of prisoners, we focus on the effects of education on the costs of operating state prisons and local jails. We use U.S. national average data to estimate the effects of education level on the probability of incarceration in state prisons or in county and municipal jails for each combination of age, race/ethnicity, and gender. We use the national average cost per inmate of operating state prison system and county and municipal jails to estimate the effects of increased educational attainment on the costs of incarceration.

We use national average operating cost estimates for public secondary and postsecondary education systems to estimate the costs of providing additional education. We assume that the costs of providing additional education to a student equal the national average operating costs per student at each level of education. We subtract the costs of providing additional education from the resulting benefits to estimate the net benefits to taxpayers from increased educational attainment.

Because the benefits to taxpayers of additional education are spread over an individual's lifetime—as he or she pays more in taxes, places fewer demands on social support programs, and does not engender incarceration costs—we estimate the expected effects of increased education over each year of an individual's lifetime and then discount the annual benefits to calculate their current values at age 18. Because much of our data are for 2002, we discount all dollar amounts to 2002 dollars, at an annual rate of 3 percent. We then estimate the net benefit of increased educational attainment to taxpayers in 2002 dollars.

Because of data limitations in the SIPP, it is not possible to estimate similar effects for immigrants—those young enough to obtain additional U.S.-based education at the high school or postsecondary level—as for the native-born. For that reason, we focus our report on results for U.S.-born individuals. However, we did include immigrants in our sample and estimated models to differentiate between native- and foreign-born individuals. While not definitive, estimates for immigrants comparable to those we present here for the native-born suggest that the benefits from increased education for immigrants will be of a similar order of magnitude.

Payments for Taxes and Social Support and Insurance Programs

Greater educational attainment increases the likelihood that an individual will be employed and the level of his or her wages or salary when employed. The available evidence strongly indicates that more education increases an employed person's earnings capacity (their wage when employed) by at least 7 to 10 percent per additional year of schooling. The higher earnings realized by more highly educated people result in higher tax payments and higher payments to social support and insurance programs.

We model tax and social support and insurance payments as a function of education level, age, and demographic characteristics. For every population group, increases in an individual's education level result in substantial increases in payments into tax and social support and insurance programs. Graduating from college rather than ending schooling with some college provides the largest impact on tax payments, followed by obtaining a high school diploma rather than dropping out of high school. The difference between the tax payments made by a person with a high school diploma and an otherwise similar person with some college is smaller, but still substantial.

The effects of increases in education on tax and social insurance payments are generally greater for men than for women at all education levels and in all race/ethnic groups.

Spending for Social Support and Insurance Programs

Because an increase in educational attainment increases both the likelihood of employment and an individual's wages when employed, it reduces the likelihood that the individual will participate in social support programs. The higher earnings resulting from greater educational attainment also reduce the amount that a more highly educated person collects when he or she does participate in most social support programs.

Analyses focused on the benefits of increased education to students or to society as a whole generally view public assistance costs as transfer payments. From this perspective, reductions in social support payments resulting from increases in educational attainment simply reduce transfers from taxpayers to social support program participants, with no benefits to society as a whole except for reductions in the administrative costs of social support programs. But, from the perspective of taxpayers, who provide the funds that social support programs distribute to participants, reductions in the costs of social support programs resulting from increased education are a benefit.

We model participation in each of eight social support programs as a function of education level, age, and demographic characteristics. Except for Unemployment Insurance and Social Security, increases in an individual's education level result in substantial reductions in the likelihood of participation and in benefits paid when the individual participates. Unemployment Insurance is an exception in that the level of compensation received depends on the person's last salary, which in turn depends on that person's level of education. Social Security is an exception in that the retirement compensation received under the retirement subprogram depends on the person's cumulative contribution during the entire time he or she spent in the work force, which in turn is highly sensitive to that individual's level of education.

The greatest reductions in spending on social support programs result from graduating from high school rather than dropping out. Beyond the high school diploma, some college has a greater impact for women and a college degree has greater impact for men.

Spending for Prisons and Jails

Research strongly demonstrates that education reduces the likelihood that an individual will engage in criminal activity. Increases in educational attainment consequently reduce the likelihood that an individual will be incarcerated. Reductions in the size of the prison and jail population decrease the costs of operating and maintaining correctional facilities. Because federal prisons hold a small share of inmates and account for a small fraction of nationwide incarceration, we concentrate on the savings that would be achieved on spending for state prisons and county and municipal jails.

Analyses of the effects of increased education on the costs of the criminal justice system often account not only for incarceration costs but also the other criminal justice system costs, such as police and adjudication. Because of resource limitation, we limited our analysis to the effects of increased education on incarceration costs.

Increases in educational attainment yield the greatest savings in incarceration costs among those who graduate from high school rather than dropping out. The savings to the public budget are less from those who have some college education rather than none, and rather little from those who graduate from college compared to settling for some college. Even for the highest-risk population subgroups of black and Hispanic men, a bachelor's degree results in just a small increase in incarceration savings compared with entering but not graduating college.

For both men and women, the primary savings on the costs of incarceration result from increased education within the black population. For each race/ethnicity group, the magnitude of savings within each female group is generally about one-tenth of that in the corresponding male group.

The Cost of Additional Education

Increasing educational attainment requires higher spending to provide the additional education. Our estimates are based on U.S. national average costs of public education.

In the 2001–2002 school year, the closest corresponding school year to the calendar year 2002, in which our data were collected, the national average current expenditure per student in average daily attendance (ADA) in public K–12 education was about $7,700. That school year, it cost taxpayers about $7,600 per full-time equivalent (FTE) student to provide additional education in a public two-year college and about $10,000 per FTE to provide additional education in a public four-year college or university.

These are the additional costs of providing additional education. They do not include the costs of programs and policies aimed at motivating students to obtain additional education.

Net Benefits to Taxpayers

The net benefits to taxpayers of increased educational attainment equal the sum of the increases in public revenues and the reductions in public spending resulting from increased education minus the cost of providing the additional education.

To illustrate the calculations: On average, increasing a U.S.-born, white man's educational attainment from less than high school graduation to high school graduation would result in increased tax payments over his lifetime equal to $54,000. (All the figures in this paragraph are presented in 2002 dollars, in discounted present value to age 18). The increase in his education level would also result in reduced future demands on social support programs and reduced future incarceration costs equal to about $22,000 and $13,000, respectively. Thus, the average total public benefits of increasing a U.S.-born, white male's education level from less than high school to high school graduate would equal about $89,000. Providing the additional education would cost about $15,000, so the net benefit to taxpayers would be about $74,000. In sum, if a U.S.-born, white male who would drop out of high school were to instead graduate high school, taxpayers would realize net benefits equal, in discounted present value, to about $74,000.

The benefits to taxpayers from increased educational attainment clearly exceed the costs of providing the additional education by a large margin for the members of every population group. Regardless of a student's gender or race/ethnicity, raising the level of education he or she attains creates high net benefits for the public budget.

Again, we note that these results pertain to the net benefits to taxpayers of increases in students' educational attainment. We do not consider the costs of developing and operating programs and policies aimed at inducing students to pursue higher education levels.

Sensitivity Analyses

To test how sensitive our results are to our estimates of the effects of increases in education level, we recalculated the benefits to taxpayers from an increase in education for each demographic group assuming that the effects of increases in education on tax payments, social program costs, and incarceration costs were each 25 percent smaller than our original estimate. Reducing the estimated effect of increasing education from less than high school to high school graduate by 25 percent resulted in a reduction in the discounted present value of lifetime net benefits to taxpayers of 28 to 34 percent, depending on the demographic group, for U.S.-born men and women. The results of similar sensitivity analyses for the effects of increasing education from high school graduate to some college and for the effect of increasing education from some college to college graduate were very similar.

The present value of net benefits to taxpayers from an increase in education are substantial even if we assume the effects of education on public revenues and costs are 25 percent smaller than our estimates. We estimate that the benefit to taxpayers from increasing an individual's education from less than high school to high school graduate is at least $51,000 (present value, net of the cost of providing the additional education) for each U.S.-born demographic group. If we assume that the effect of increasing education from high school graduate to some college is 25 percent smaller than our estimate, the benefit to taxpayers is still at least $24,000 (present value, net of the cost of providing the additional education), depending on the demographic group. For the increase in education from some college to college graduate, the benefit to taxpayers, assuming a 25-percent-smaller effect of education level, is at least $53,000 (present value, net of the cost of providing the additional education), depending on the demographic group.

Putting the Results in Perspective

As noted previously, we use data collected in 2002 to estimate the models used in this analysis. In doing so, we assume that the estimated relationships between education level and governmental revenues and costs will remain approximately the same into the future. Specifically, we assume that the effects of education on earnings and, consequently, on tax payments and participation in social programs, in the future will be essentially the same as the effects observed in 2002. We also assume that federal, state, and local tax structures, social support programs, and incarceration patterns will not change substantially in the future.

Changes in some of these relationships are likely to occur at some future date. Consequently, the estimates presented here cannot be viewed as precise. However, the magnitudes of the estimates are generally so large that, even if changes in these relationships substantially reduce the effects of increased educational attainment on government revenues and costs, the net benefits to taxpayers will still be substantial. Moreover, changes that increase the effects of education level on government revenues and costs are more likely than are changes that reduce the effects. If such changes occur, the estimates presented here will understate the effects of increased educational attainment on government revenues and costs.

Our analysis assumes that the relationships observed in the data are causal. That is, we assume that the differences in contributions to government revenues and costs between more highly educated and less highly educated people are the result of the differences in their levels of education. There is abundant evidence that increased educational attainment leads to increases in earnings and that earnings are related to contributions to government revenues and costs. It is possible that some other factor is related to both the level of an individual's education and his or her contributions to government revenues and costs. But it is clear that education is a dominant factor, even if there are others. Moreover, the magnitude of the effect of education on earnings has grown consistently over time. Because we assume that the relationships between educational attainment and contributions to government revenues and costs that existed in 2002 will continue over time, our estimates do not reflect the effects of increases in the effect of educational attainment on earnings and, consequently, on government revenues and costs.

The bottom line is that these estimates, notwithstanding the inherent uncertainties in estimating future trends and patterns, show that increased educational attainment yields significant benefits to taxpayers. We recognize that the greatest gains accrue to those whose education levels are improved and that increases in educational attainment also provide numerous types of noneconomic benefits in addition to economic benefits. However, this analysis indicates that raising an individual's level of education creates high benefits for the public budget, benefits that should be considered in assessing the importance of finding, funding, and implementing programs aimed at increasing educational attainment.

Acknowledgments

We are indebted to several RAND colleagues who contributed to this study. Richard Neu, J. R. Lockwood, and Lynn Karoly reviewed earlier drafts of this report. Their insightful comments and suggestions provided significant contributions to this analysis. We also thank Shelley Wiseman for helping us with the structure and clarity of this report, Nancy Good and Christopher Dirks for helping with the preparation of this report, and James Torr, whose editorial expertise greatly improved the overall quality of this report.

Abbreviations

ADA	average daily attendance
CPS	Current Population Survey
EITC	Earned Income Tax Credit
FTE	full-time equivalent
GED	General Educational Development credential
HSG	high school graduate
HUD	U.S. Department of Housing and Urban Development
OLS	ordinary least squares
SIPP	Survey of Income and Program Participation
SSI	Supplemental Security Income

CHAPTER ONE

Introduction

The Problem

Policymakers in most states face a fundamental challenge—motivating taxpayers to provide the funds required to meet the mounting educational needs of the nation's population. This challenge is driven by major economic and social waves shaping the nation. The level of education that an individual needs to be competitive in the workplace has been increasing for the past 20 years.[1] The high-paying industrial jobs that used to be available to people who lacked even a high school diploma have largely disappeared. The service-related jobs taking their place require a level of knowledge and skill that require a high school diploma at a minimum. And many jobs can be obtained only after completing programs offered at colleges and universities. High school graduation and preferably some postsecondary education have effectively become minimum requirements for rewarding employment.

At the same time, significant and growing segments of the U.S. population have traditionally experienced relatively low levels of educational attainment. If current trends continue, an increasing fraction of the population will lack the education needed to succeed in the labor market.

K–12 public school spending as a percentage of personal income has declined since the mid-1970s (Carroll et al., 2005). And studies have suggested that higher education systems also face mounting fiscal challenges (Benjamin and Carroll, 1997). K–12 schools and postsecondary institutions across the country face budgetary restrictions.

Meeting anticipated demands and expanding educational attainment will be expensive. Quite reasonably, taxpayers and their representatives ask why they should contribute more to the support of educational institutions. Shouldn't those who directly benefit from more schooling pay their own way? And if they choose not to invest in their own education, isn't that their problem? Until good answers can be provided to such questions, it will be difficult to convince federal, state, and local policymakers that they should make the investments necessary to increase students' educational attainment.

---

[1] See, for example, Johnson and Reed, 2007.

Research Objective

Discussions of programs and policies that can affect students' educational attainment often focus on the consequences for students and for society as a whole. We do not question the relevance of those perspectives. However, taxpayers who do not have children in school or who do not see their well-being as tightly linked to the quality of the labor force may object to supporting programs and policies that do not benefit them directly. Our objective is to demonstrate that programs and policies that result in increased educational attainment provide benefits to all taxpayers, even those who do not have children in school. We show that, totally aside from the benefits that accrue to individuals who increase their educational attainment, taxpayers reap significant benefits from other people's increases in educational attainment.[2] These benefits should be considered in discussions of public investments in education.

We do not suggest that policies and programs ought to be adopted or rejected solely because of their effects on taxpayers. But we do suggest that taxpayers will realize some benefits from programs and policies that increase students' education levels and should, consequently, take account of these benefits in considering policy options.

The Costs of Providing Education Versus the Overall Costs of Increasing Educational Attainment

In Chapter Seven, we provide estimates of the benefits that increases in educational attainment have for taxpayers, net of the cost of providing the additional education (we discuss such costs in Chapter Six). However, programs and policies that seek to increase students' educational attainment must not just *provide* the additional education, but also *motivate* students to pursues and complete the additional education. An important limit on the scope of our study is that we do not consider either the kinds of programs or policies that would be needed to induce individuals to stay in school longer or the costs of such programs or policies. We consider only the benefits to taxpayers when an individual's education is increased.

Because we do not account for the costs of programs that induce individuals to pursue higher levels of education, our study is not a cost-benefit analysis. We do not suggest that benefits to taxpayers of such programs will necessarily exceed their costs, and it is certainly possible that they may not. A cost-benefit analysis of a program aimed at increasing educational attainment would have to consider several complexities. One such complexity is that the program would not be perfectly effective: Some program

---

[2] In the context of cost-savings or cost-benefit analysis, our objective is the equivalent of calculating the "shadow price," or the economic value (positive or negative) for taxpayers of increasing an individual's educational attainment. In this case, we focus on the shadow price solely from the perspective of taxpayers, as would be the case in a cost-savings analysis, rather than the full economic value to society, as would be estimated in a cost-benefit analysis. For further discussion of shadow prices in the context of cost-savings and cost-benefit analysis of social programs, see Karoly (2008).

participants will not attain a higher level of education despite their participation. As an example, a program aimed at increasing the likelihood that students will achieve a high school diploma rather than dropping out may involve both students who would have completed high school had they not participated in the program and students who drop out despite their participation. Any cost-benefit analysis would have to recognize that only those participants whose education level is affected by the program will generate additional benefits to taxpayers, whereas all participants will engender costs. A second complexity is that a cost-benefit analysis would have to consider the benefits to program participants and other nonparticipants, such as participants' parents, and to society as a whole as well as benefits to taxpayers.

Again, our objective is to examine one part of that broader calculation: the existence and magnitude of taxpayer benefits when an individual's education is increased. We leave to others the comparison of the costs of a specific program to its benefits for all stakeholders. Moreover, we do not offer a position on state support for education. We seek only to estimate the benefits that taxpayers—even those who do not have children in school—realize from increases in educational attainment.

Research Questions

In this study, we explore the benefits of increased educational attainment for taxpayers. We recognize that the greatest gains accrue to those whose education levels are improved and that increases in educational attainment also provide numerous types of noneconomic benefits in addition to economic benefits. However, we concentrate on three types of economic benefits to those who would have to pay the costs of policies and programs aimed at raising educational attainment. Specifically, we estimate the extent to which increased education results in

- increases in federal, state, and local tax revenues and in contributions to social support and insurance programs such as Social Security and Medicare
- reductions in public expenditures on social support and insurance programs
- reductions in public expenditures on incarceration—the costs of building and operating state prisons and county and municipal jails.

We use national data to estimate the relationships between an individual's increased educational attainment and his or her contributions to public revenues, expenditures, and incarceration costs. We then use these estimates to compute the discounted present value of the effects that the increase in an individual's educational attainment has on the public budget—effects that would be incurred over the individual's lifetime—to estimate the benefits to taxpayers of the increase in the individual's educational attainment.

We discount all dollar values to age 18. That is, we calculate the discounted present value, in 2002 dollars, of the estimated streams of contributions to and draws on the public budget at age 18 for an individual given his or her level of schooling and demographic group. We assume the appropriate discount rate is 3 percent per year.

Different segments of the population participate at different rates in social support programs. For example, some social support programs, such as Temporary Assistance to Needy Families and the Supplemental Nutrition Assistance Program,[3] have traditionally served low-income women with young children. Consequently, an increase in the education of a woman will, on average, more greatly reduce welfare payments than will an equal increase in the education of a man. In contrast, the effect of education on incarceration rates and consequent costs is more marked for men because very few women, regardless of education level, are incarcerated. Therefore, we conducted separate analyses for eight different population groups distinguished by gender and race/ethnicity—African-American (black), Asian, Hispanic, and non-Hispanic white (white).

To generate our estimates, we use data from the Survey of Income and Program Participation (SIPP) (U.S. Census Bureau, 2005a, 2005b, 2005c), which provides, for each individual, his or her education level and place of birth (U.S.-born or immigrant). However, the SIPP data do not indicate an immigrant's age (or year) of arrival, where an immigrant was educated, or an immigrant's English-language proficiency. Thus, it is not possible with the SIPP data to estimate the effect of increased education for immigrants young enough to obtain additional U.S.-based education at the high school or post-secondary level on such outcomes as taxes paid, benefits received, and incarceration costs. For that reason, we focus our report on results for U.S.-born individuals.

However, we did include immigrants in our sample, and we estimated models to differentiate between U.S.- and foreign-born individuals. While not definitive, estimates for immigrants comparable to those we present here for the native-born suggest that the benefits from increased education for immigrants will be of a similar order of magnitude. However, more-precise estimates of the effects of additional schooling for immigrants will require data as rich as the SIPP but with information on where an immigrant was educated and his or her English-language proficiency.

The SIPP includes a nationally representative sample of the U.S. population. It includes some, but very few, Native Americans. Because we want the empirical estimates to reflect the relationships between education level and government revenues and costs for the U.S. population as a whole, we include Native Americans in the estimates. However, because there are so few Native Americans in the sample, we cannot be sure that the specific results for that group accurately reflect the experience of Native Americans. Accordingly, we do not present estimates of the effects of increased edu-

---

[3] As of October 1, 2008, this is the new name for the federal Food Stamps Program.

cation among Native Americans' on their contributions to government revenues and costs.

Our analytic approach as it relates to the specific research questions is described in more detail in subsequent chapters of this report.

Illustrative Examples

The following examples illustrate the ways in which the results presented here might bear on policy decisions. The examples are hypothetical, but they are based on analyses of actual educational programs and policies.

First, consider a one-year preschool program that serves disadvantaged children and costs the government $5,000 per child. Suppose a rigorous evaluation of the program demonstrates that it results in a number of positive outcomes, one of which is a 10-percentage-point increase in participants' high school graduation rate. (Many of the children in the program would have completed high school even if they had not been involved in the program. And some of the children in the program drop out of high school despite their participation in the program.) The issue is how to place a monetary value to taxpayers on that outcome.

We could estimate the present value of the difference in the taxes paid by a high school graduate versus a high school dropout over his or her lifetime. We could similarly estimate the present value of the lifetime differences in expenditures by social support programs and in incarceration costs between a high school graduate and a high school dropout. However, we would also need to account for the fact that when a student stays in school rather than dropping out, taxpayers would have to pay for the additional years of schooling, and we would have to subtract the cost of those additional years of schooling from the benefits that accrue from higher educational attainment.

Let's say that the resulting estimate of the present value to taxpayers of a high school graduate over a high school dropout is $80,000. Suppose $5,000 is spent on every child in the preschool program. Because the program causes only 10 percent of the children to reach the higher education level, the present value benefit to taxpayers of the program is $8,000 per child included in the program compared with the program cost of $5,000 per child.

Second, consider a program at the high school level emphasizing small learning communities, long-term student-teacher relationships, and a rigorous curriculum. Suppose such a program were found to increase high school graduation rates 16 percentage points at a cost of $6,000 per child. The effects on the public budget resulting from inducing a student to complete high school rather than dropping out is the same, an increase of $80,000, present value. In this hypothetical example, because the high school–based program caused 16 percent of the children to reach the higher education level, the present value benefit to taxpayers of the program is $12,800 per child included in the program compared with the program cost of $6,000 per child.

Note that we do not consider other benefits to taxpayers that might result from either example program. For example, a preschool program might reduce the rate of grade repetition or the use of special education, saving the associated costs to the schools and, consequently, to the taxpayers. A rigorous high school program might reduce substance abuse among participants, reducing public health and police costs. We omit these benefits to taxpayers because they are unique to the particular intervention and would not apply to alternatives.

However, notwithstanding the benefits to taxpayers that are unique to either example, many of the principal effects of increasing a student's education are the same for both. More generally, there are a large number of possible programs and policies that might affect students' educational attainment. Our objective is not to focus on any particular policy or program, but, rather, to note that taxpayers will benefit from a successful policy or program and, therefore, taxpayers should consider the merits of proposals even if they do not have children in school.

Note, also, that these examples do not require that we value, as would be the case in a cost-benefit analysis, the private benefits to participants in either program, such as higher lifetime earnings or other benefits that accrue from greater educational attainment. Nor must we value the private benefits to nonparticipants from the improved outcomes of participants, such as lower rates of crime and the reductions in the associated pecuniary and nonpecuniary crime victim costs.

Third, consider an example focused on the effects of a proposed decrease in school funding. Governor Arnold Schwarzenegger of California has proposed a budget for fiscal 2009 that would cut state higher education funding by roughly $300 million. This cut in higher education funding, coupled with planned increases in student fees, could deny access to more than 9,000 students at the University of California (UC) and more than 18,000 students at California State University (CSU). Some of those denied access to the state's public four-year colleges and universities will attend private schools or community colleges, which cannot restrict the enrollment of eligible students. However, community colleges also face significant funding cuts under the proposed budget. Funding cuts, coupled with increased enrollments by students who would otherwise have enrolled in UC or CSU, will result in significant reductions in the classes and support services available to students in community colleges and, consequently, in both the proportion of community college entrants who complete a two-year program and in the proportion of students who continue on to a bachelor's degree. Suppose the budget cuts were enacted and, as a result 5,000 fewer students completed some college and 5,000 fewer students completed a bachelor's degree. If the present-value benefits to taxpayers of some college are and a bachelor's degree are $40,000 and $75,000 per student, respectively, the proposed budget cuts would save taxpayers about $300 million, but cost taxpayers future benefits of which the present value is about $575 million.

Here too, we do not value, as would be the case in a cost-benefit analysis, reductions in private benefits to students whose education levels would be reduced by the budget cuts, such as higher lifetime earnings or other benefits that accrue from greater educational attainment, nor do we value the costs to society resulting from a less well-educated labor force. Rather, we note that taxpayers who do not have children likely to attend college and who feel that the students who benefit from increased education ought to bear the costs of those increases will still lose benefits when budgets are cut and students' access to education is consequently reduced.

Previous Research

There have been numerous analyses of programs aimed at improving some aspect of the quality of education. Some of these programs are designed to increase students' education levels. Others are designed to improve some other aspect of the quality of education, but they also affect students' education levels. However, these analyses generally focus on the effects that the program being evaluated has on the students involved, including increases in their educational attainment and, sometimes, on their families and the society more generally. Such analyses generally do not examine the programs' effects on taxpayers in detail.

Also, analyses focused on the benefits of increased education to the students or to society as a whole generally view public assistance costs as transfer payments. An increase in a student's education reduces the likelihood that he or she will participate in social support programs and, consequently, reduces social support program costs. From the perspective of society as a whole, this simply means that fewer funds are transferred from taxpayers to beneficiaries. The only consequent savings from this perspective are reductions in the administrative costs of social support programs. But, from the perspective of taxpayers, who provide the funds that social support program distribute to participants, the reductions in the costs of social support programs resulting from increased education are a benefit.

Krop (1998) conducted analyses similar to ours. However, his specific results are not directly comparable with ours, for two reasons. First, because his objective was to estimate the effects of increasing black and Hispanic education levels to that of whites, he reported the aggregate effects of increasing black and Hispanic education levels on government costs and revenues for the entire U.S. population of blacks and Hispanics born in 1990. He did not report the effects of increases in education on an individual's contributions to and draws on public budgets. Second, Krop examined the effects of increased education on the costs of the social support programs in effect in 1991. The 1996 Personal Responsibility and Work Opportunity Reconciliation Act and the 1997

Balanced Budget Act dramatically restructured the social support system, eliminating some programs, introducing some new programs, and imposing more-stringent eligibility rules and lifetime-total and one-time caps on participation in the income-support programs that were continued.

Although Krop's empirical results cannot be directly compared with ours, his general findings are suggestive. He found that increases in education yield substantial increases in tax revenues and in contributions to social support programs and substantial reductions in public spending for social support programs and incarceration.

Belfield and Levin (2007) estimate the effects of graduating from high school rather than dropping out on public revenues and costs, focusing on California. They distinguish between men and women by race/ethnicity for whites, blacks, and Hispanics. They do not consider place of birth. They assume that students who are induced to graduate from high school rather than dropping out will continue on to college at a rate equal to the national average rate of college continuation by those in the lowest quartile of academic achievement, and the researchers compare estimates for high school dropouts with those for high school graduates without differentiating level of education above high school. Consequently, their results are not directly comparable with our estimates.

Belfield and Levin estimate the effects of completing high school on the present value of lifetime federal and California state and local tax revenues. Their estimate of the present value, in 2005 dollars, of the additional federal state and local tax payments resulting from high school graduation rather than dropping out is about $101,000. The increase in tax payments resulting from high school graduation ranges from about $49,000 for black women to about $182,000 for white men.

Belfield and Levin examine the effects of high school completion on federal, state, and local (California) spending on three welfare programs and on the costs of crime, including spending on the criminal justice system, corrections, crime prevention, and publicly provided health care. Because they do not consider seven of the ten social support programs that we examine, their estimates of the effects of completing high school on social support program costs are not comparable with ours. And, because we consider only the effects of increased educational attainment on incarceration costs and do not consider the other types of crime-related costs to taxpayers that Belfield and Levin include in their analysis, their estimates of the effects of completing high school on crime-related costs are not comparable with ours.

Rouse (2005) estimates the effects of graduating from high school, rather than dropping out, on federal and national average state income tax payments and Social Security payments. She compares total tax payments by high school dropouts with tax payments for high school graduates and with tax payments by individuals who have a high school diploma or greater level of education. She presents estimates for each of three different assumptions regarding future annual earnings growth and for each of three different discount rates. However, she does not distinguish among gender, race/ethnicity, or place of birth.

Assuming 0 percent annual growth in earnings and a 3.5 percent discount rate, Rouse estimates that the effect of completing high school, rather than dropping out, on the discounted present value (2004 dollars) of federal and state income taxes paid is about $42,000 and that the effect on total income and Social Security taxes paid is about $70,000. The corresponding estimates for high school graduate or more schooling are about $104,000 in federal and state income taxes and about $155,000 for total income and Social Security taxes.

In addition to these studies focusing specifically on the economic value of raising educational attainment, efforts have been made, in various cost-benefit studies of social programs, to attach an overall value to raising an individual's level of education, either in terms of benefits to taxpayers or to society as a whole. For example, Masse and Barnett (2002), Reynolds et al. (2002), and Karoly and Bigelow (2005) estimate the economic value of the higher educational attainment, measured for participants in various high-quality preschool programs relative to program nonparticipants.

Aos et al. (2004) also estimate the value of higher educational attainment in their cost-benefit analysis of an array of early intervention and prevention programs for children and youth. In terms of taxpayer benefits, these studies account primarily for the effect of increased years of schooling on income and payroll taxes, a more limited set of benefits than we account for in this study. Moreover, these studies typically do not report the estimated economic values associated with raising education levels that they employ in their cost-benefit analyses.

Definition of Terms

Research has traditionally measured education in terms of years of schooling completed. However, in this study, we concentrate on the level of education received by an individual instead of years completed. The levels we consider are as follows:

- **Less than high school education.** Because federal law requires that young people go to school until they are 16 years old, most individuals who choose to end their schooling before high school graduation have completed at least their sophomore year. On the other hand, some may complete most of their senior year before leaving high school. For this study, a high school dropout is any individual who does not earn a high school diploma or a General Educational Development credential (GED).
- **High school graduate.** An individual of any age who earns a high school diploma or a GED but does not go on to college is a high school graduate.

- **Some college.** An individual who earns some college credits but does not earn a (typically four-year) bachelor's degree. Individuals with some college may have earned a (typically two-year) associate's degree.
- **College graduate.** An individual who earns a bachelor's degree or more.

We chose to concentrate on levels of education rather than years of schooling for several reasons. First, beginning in the 1980s, the Census Bureau adopted a degree-based system for the Census and the Current Population Survey (CPS). Our use of a level-of-education approach will enhance the comparability of our study with research that uses Census and CPS data. Second, we believe that today's labor market places greater value on degrees than it does on the underlying number of years of education. In an economy in which clerical tasks are increasingly automated and delegated to computers and in which many, or even most, new jobs are created in technology sectors, receiving a college degree matters much more than making the jump from 15 years of schooling to 16—even if they amount to the same thing. Our key data source, the SIPP, collects education data by level of education and degrees obtained as well as years of education.

We use the terms *educational attainment* and *education level* to refer to the level of schooling that an individual completes. This study is not about "better" education in the sense of schools doing a better job. In our analysis, we treat all benefits as incremental and relative to the respective baseline of the increase in attainment. For instance, if we want to assess the benefit to taxpayers of a student earning a high school diploma rather than dropping out, the benefit is the difference in expected tax payments, social program costs, and the costs of incarceration between the average high school graduate and the average high school dropout, and not simply the expected values for high school graduates *per se*. We apply a similar logic to all costs and benefits.

We use the term *benefits to taxpayers* to refer to the benefits that taxpayers gain when an individual completes a higher level of schooling. In this study, we focus on benefits to taxpayers; we do not consider either the direct, or private, benefits from educational attainment that students obtain from an increase in their education, nor do we consider either the private or social benefits that accrue to the society as a whole when an individual completes a higher level of schooling.

Organization of the Report

This report is organized as follows. Chapter Two outlines our approach to the analyses. Chapter Three examines the relationships between educational attainment and tax revenues and contributions to social support and insurance programs. Chapter Four examines the relationships between educational attainment and spending on social support and insurance programs. Chapter Five examines the relationships between educational attainment and spending for prisons and jails. Chapter Six presents estimates of the costs of providing additional education. Chapter Seven calculates the benefits to taxpayers from increases in educational attainment. Chapter Eight summarizes our findings.

We also include several appendixes. Appendix A describes the data used in the analyses. Appendix B presents the empirical analyses used to estimate the effects of increased educational attainment on tax payments. Appendix C presents the empirical analyses used to estimate the effects of increased educational attainment on participation in social programs and the resulting costs. Appendix D presents the empirical analyses used to estimate the effects of increased educational attainment on incarceration and the resulting costs.

CHAPTER TWO
Analytic Approach

There is abundant evidence that people with more schooling earn higher wages and salaries. There is also evidence that more highly educated people are more likely to be employed and to work full-time when employed. A direct result of higher earnings and greater employment is increased income and, consequently, increased payments in income taxes and "consumption" taxes, such as sales, real estate, and excise taxes. Also, individuals with higher incomes are more likely to succeed using their own resources and, consequently, less likely to use social support systems. Finally, individuals better able to support themselves are less likely to resort to crime and, consequently, less likely to be incarcerated.

We use a nationally representative sample of roughly 40,000 individuals covered in all months of 2002 by the SIPP (U.S. Census Bureau, 2005a, 2005b, 2005c) to estimate the relationships between education level and various government revenues and costs.[1] We use the estimated relationships between education level and various government revenues and costs to project the effects of increases in an individual's educational attainment on governmental revenues and costs over the individual's lifetime. In doing so, we assume that the estimated relationships between education level and governmental revenues and costs observed in 2002 will remain approximately the same into the future.

In projecting the effects of increasing an individual's education, we estimate his or her contributions to and draws on public revenues from age 18 through age 79. We assume that all schooling occurs consecutively and that the effects of an individual's educational attainment begin immediately on completion of schooling. For example, we assume that a high school graduate attends school through age 17 and interacts with the public budget from age 18 onward.

Independent Variables

The independent variables in the models described below are

---

[1] Appendix A describes the data.

- a set of dummy variables indicating the level of educational attainment:
  - less than high school graduate
  - high school graduate
  - some college
  - bachelor's degree or more
- age and age-squared
- interactions between educational attainment variables and age variables
- a set of race/ethnicity dummies for Asians, blacks, Hispanics, and whites
- a dummy variable for immigrant status.

Age is included as quadratic to allow for the nonlinear effects of age, particularly as it relates to cumulative experience in the labor market. Further, age and education status are interacted to allow for the slope on educational attainment to vary with age.

In all regressions, the intercept refers to the reference case of a U.S.-born, white individual who graduated from high school.

We run separate models for men and women, consistent with human-capital models of labor market outcomes. The fact that there are only small subsamples prevents us from running models for groups based on race/ethnicity.

Education and Earnings

The labor-market benefit of more education is one of the most-researched and best-documented relationships in social science: People with more schooling earn higher wages and salaries.[2] We reviewed the literature related to the effects of educational attainment on earning capacity. We compiled the results of 27 studies that contain some 96 different effect-of-education calculations.[3]

These studies generally address the effects that education has on an individual's productivity as reflected in the wage or salary he or she commands in the labor market. The research generally focus on what an individual earns while employed full-time. The studies generally do not consider the effects of education on *whether* an individual is employed and, if so, whether full- or part-time. Accordingly, they generally do not consider the effects of education on *income*; instead they focus on *earnings capacity*, in the sense of what someone earns when employed full-time.

The studies we reviewed used somewhat different methodologies and different database. Nonetheless, there is substantial agreement among them regarding the

---

[2] See Card (1999) for an extensive review of the literature and a discussion of numerous empirical studies.

[3] The studies we reviewed are listed in the references.

effects of education on earnings capacity. All agree that increases in education resulted in increases in earnings capacity. While the results differ slightly depending on the approach and data, the common finding is that an additional year of schooling leads, on average, to an increase of 7–10 percent in earnings capacity.

Card (1999) provides a thorough review of related economics literature, focusing on models and estimation results from several different estimation approaches. He also finds that studies generally agree that education has a positive causal effect on earnings capacity. In a separate, more recent review of the benefits of education, Krueger and Lindahl (2001) conclude that each additional year of schooling appears to raise earnings capacity by about 10 percent.

Calculations of the effect of education level on earnings capacity have been challenged on the grounds that the calculations are biased. Specifically, some critics maintain that individuals with greater ability (e.g., because of greater intelligence or more aggressive attitudes) choose to obtain more education, and so it is the fact that they have greater ability in the first place, rather than their additional education, that accounts for their higher earnings capacity. However, studies generally find a *higher* impact of education on earnings capacity, instead of a lower one, when taking into account such potential biases. These tests for causality include studies that include data on attitudes and other factors that could influence earnings capacity and studies of twins and siblings that completed different levels of education (Rouse, 2005). These studies find, for example, that persons with high innate ability who terminate their education at a low level, possibly because of family financial circumstances, do better in the labor market than others with lesser ability who complete the same level of schooling. Conversely, persons with low ability who drift through several levels of schooling tend to earn less than others with higher ability who complete the same level of schooling. This strongly suggests that education does have a causal effect on earnings capacity, whether we consider personal ability or not.

Estimates of the effect of education level on earnings capacity, using "simple" methods that do not take into account potential ability and background bias, range from 2 to 11 percent greater earnings capacity per year of schooling and cluster around 7 percent. Estimates that take those biases into account find that each additional year of schooling increases earnings capacity by 5 to 14 percent and cluster around 10 percent. For example, Ashenfelter, Harmon, and Oosterbeek (1999) find a 6.6 percent and 9.3 percent increase in earnings capacity using simple and advanced methods, respectively.

Most of these studies that we reviewed were completed in the 1990s and used data from the 1980s and 1990s. Because the differences in the wages and salaries paid to persons with different levels of schooling have generally increased over time, these studies' estimates understate the current effects of education level on earnings. Table 2.1 shows the ratios of median weekly earnings by educational attainment for men and

Table 2.1
Ratio of Median Usual Weekly Earnings of Full-time Wage and Salary Workers 25 Years and Over, by Educational Attainment

Year	Men			Women		
	High School Graduate to Less Than High School Graduate	Some College to High School Graduate	Bachelor's Degree or More to Some College	High School Graduate to Less Than High School Graduate	Some College to High School Graduate	Bachelor's Degree or More to Some College
1979	1.22	1.07	1.20	1.22	1.14	1.25
1980	1.22	1.09	1.19	1.23	1.15	1.26
1981	1.24	1.09	1.22	1.24	1.18	1.25
1982	1.28	1.10	1.22	1.28	1.16	1.26
1983	1.29	1.09	1.23	1.26	1.17	1.28
1984	1.30	1.12	1.26	1.30	1.18	1.28
1985	1.30	1.16	1.25	1.33	1.18	1.31
1986	1.30	1.17	1.27	1.33	1.19	1.32
1987	1.31	1.17	1.31	1.35	1.20	1.34
1988	1.32	1.15	1.35	1.35	1.21	1.35
1989	1.30	1.15	1.36	1.32	1.25	1.34
1990	1.32	1.18	1.37	1.31	1.25	1.35
1991	1.35	1.20	1.36	1.31	1.25	1.37
1992	1.36	1.16	1.43	1.32	1.21	1.46
1993	1.37	1.17	1.41	1.32	1.22	1.45
1994	1.45	1.18	1.41	1.37	1.21	1.50
1995	1.46	1.18	1.42	1.36	1.20	1.51
1996	1.45	1.17	1.45	1.36	1.21	1.49
1997	1.47	1.16	1.44	1.37	1.21	1.46
1998	1.46	1.15	1.46	1.40	1.20	1.49
1999	1.47	1.15	1.47	1.40	1.20	1.52
2000	1.46	1.17	1.48	1.38	1.20	1.50
2001	1.45	1.19	1.48	1.40	1.17	1.51
2002	1.47	1.18	1.49	1.41	1.19	1.49
2003	1.46	1.18	1.53	1.44	1.18	1.49
2004	1.45	1.18	1.50	1.46	1.18	1.49
2005	1.43	1.17	1.52	1.45	1.19	1.50
2006	1.45	1.17	1.51	1.40	1.20	1.50

SOURCE: Current Population Survey, U.S. Department of Labor, Bureau of Labor Statistics, Data file on median weekly earnings, 2007.

NOTE: Since 1992, data on educational attainment have been based on the "highest diploma or degree received" rather than the "number of years of school completed."

women employed full-time for 1976–2006. These data are not available separated by race/ethnicity.

The ratios have consistently increased slowly over time. Since 1976, for both men and women, the average wages and salaries paid to full-time workers at one level of education have increased more rapidly than the average wages and salaries paid workers at the next lower education level. The effects of education level on how much employed workers are paid has clearly increased over time. Consequently, the estimates cited above almost certainly understate the effects of education level on earnings capacity.

Further, as noted earlier, the studies of the effect of education on earnings capacity generally focus on how the level of education affects the wages and salaries paid to individuals who are employed full-time. They generally do not examine the effects of education on whether an individual is employed and, if so, on a full-time basis. Higher earnings capacity implies that the opportunity costs of not participating in the labor market or working part-time rather than full-time are greater. So, the positive effect of education level on earnings capacity will also increase the incentive to seek employment, particularly full-time employment.

Table 2.2 shows the annual average percentage of the population in each gender, race/ethnicity, and education level who were employed over the 1992–2007 period.[4]

Table 2.2
Percentage of Persons Age 25 to 64 Who Are Employed, by Race/Ethnicity, Gender, and Education Level, 1992–2007

		Highest Level of Education			
Race/Ethnicity	Gender	Less Than High School Graduate	High School Graduate	Some College	Bachelor's Degree or More
Asian	Female	34	53	64	67
	Male	56	73	77	84
Black	Female	29	59	71	79
	Male	41	69	77	83
Hispanic	Female	36	59	69	73
	Male	72	82	84	87
White	Female	28	52	65	72
	Male	54	72	78	82
Total	Female	28	53	65	72
	Male	52	72	78	83

SOURCE: U.S. Census Bureau and Bureau of Labor Statistics, Current Population Survey, data file on employment status, age 25 and over, by education, sex, and race, 1992–2007.

---

[4] Data on the percentage of Asians employed are only available for 1999–2007.

The available data do not distinguish between part-time and full-time employment or between U.S.-born and immigrants.

There is little variation over time and no trend over time in the employment percentages for each race/ethnicity and gender group.

It is clear that more highly educated people are more likely to be employed, regardless of race/ethnicity or gender. This is no surprise. Because more highly educated people are generally paid more, their opportunity cost of not seeking employment is greater. The higher wages paid to more highly educated people show that they are more valued by employers and, consequently, more likely to find work when they seek employment.

The available data clearly show that more highly educated people are both more likely to be employed and, when employed, paid higher wages and salaries. Hence, more highly educated people have higher incomes.

Tax Payments

Increases in income result in increases in federal, state, and local tax revenues and in contributions to social support and insurance programs, such as Social Security and Medicare. We develop separate models to estimate the effects of education on federal tax payments, on state and local tax payments, and on contributions to Social Security and Medicare. Because of the substantial differences between men and women in employment status and wages and salaries earned when employed, we develop separate models for men and women.

Federal Income Taxes

Federal income taxes are paid by families (consisting of one or more individuals) out of family income, regardless of any particular family member's income. Therefore, we use a reduced form ordinary least squares (OLS) regression approach. Rather than estimating a family's income and then their tax payments, given their income, we use family income data from the 2002 administrations of the SIPP and 2002 taxation rates by income group (Parisi, 2004–2005) to estimate federal income tax payment on a family basis. We divide this amount by the number of adults in the family to compute tax payments by individuals. We then model payments as a function of education level, age, and demographic characteristics (gender, place of birth, and race/ethnicity). We forecast payments throughout the entire working life of an adult, using appropriate survival rates, to estimate the differential impact of education level on public revenues in each year of an individual's life. We then discount the annual estimates to 2002 to estimate the present value (2002 dollars) of the impact of an increase in education on federal tax payments.

State and Local Taxes

State and local taxes are estimated like federal income taxes. We assume that such taxes are also paid out of total family income. Hence, state tax payment estimations also consist of a single regression. We calculate state and local tax payments by applying average national tax rates to pre-transfer family income reported in the SIPP. Similar to federal taxes, state tax payments are also evenly divided among the adults in the household for the OLS regression.

Payroll Taxes

Social Security and the hospital insurance portion of Medicare are financed by taxes levied on individual earnings. Not every individual pays these taxes; only the employed pay. Therefore, we use a two-part model to estimate payroll taxes. In the first step, we fit a probit model to estimate the likelihood that an individual will have positive earnings and will, therefore, pay payroll taxes. In the second step, we use an OLS model to estimate the amount of payroll taxes paid, conditional on having positive earnings. Payroll tax payment for every individual is calculated by applying the statutory payroll tax rates to individual earnings data in the SIPP. The specific response variable in the OLS is the logarithm of assumed payroll tax payments.

Social Program Participation and Costs

We estimate the effects of increases in educational attainment on social support program spending in each of the eight largest social support and insurance programs for which sufficient data on program participation and spending are available. These include

- welfare programs (Temporary Assistance to Needy Families, general assistance, and other welfare)
- subsidized housing (public housing and rental assistance)
- food stamps (the Supplemental Nutrition Assistance Program)
- Supplemental Security Income (SSI)
- Medicaid
- Medicare
- Unemployment Insurance
- Social Security (retirement, disability, and survivor programs).

These programs can be broadly divided into two categories: (1) social support programs that provide cash and noncash benefits to members of low-income households and (2) social insurance programs that replace the lost income of people who cannot work because of old age, disability, severance, etc.

Major social support programs include Temporary Assistance for Needy Families, Housing Subsidies, food stamps, SSI, and Medicaid. The decision to participate in a social support program is dictated by a comparison of the benefits available from that program and the earnings forgone in the labor market. The more educated the individual, the more he or she can command in the labor market. Therefore, increased educational attainment makes social support program participation less attractive. Also, eligibility for participation in most social support programs is limited to low-income individuals. Therefore, increases in educational attainment lead to higher incomes, which, in turn, reduce the likelihood of eligibility.

Major social insurance programs include Medicare, Unemployment Insurance, and Social Security (retirement, disability, and survivor programs). Eligibility for some social insurance programs depends on having been employed for some period of time, and the amount of benefits provided to a beneficiary sometimes depends on the amounts paid into the program by the beneficiary or on behalf of the beneficiary. Because more highly educated individuals are more likely to be employed and likely to earn more when employed, they are more likely to qualify for social insurance and likely to receive higher benefits when they draw on the program.

The SIPP provides data on the amount of benefit received by the individual or family for welfare and food stamps and at the individual level for Unemployment Insurance, SSI, and Social Security.[5] In each of these programs, we use a two-part model to assess the effect of educational attainment on program benefits.[6] In the first stage, we estimate a probit model of program utilization as a function of educational attainment, age, and individual characteristics. In the second stage, for those who are program participants, we model the logarithm of annual income from the particular program as a function of educational attainment, age, and individual characteristics. Finally we combine results from both models to derive program benefits by education level.

The data indicate whether an individual lives in assisted housing. For subsidized housing, we use data from the U.S. Department of Housing and Urban Development (HUD) on total annual program cost and number of residents covered. We assume that unit housing cost per person is constant across education levels and demographic groups. This makes a single-part model, in which housing-subsidy utilization depends on education level, age, and other variables, sufficient. Then, the expected housing subsidy is equal to likelihood of utilization as predicted by the single-part model times average program cost per person.

We use two-part models for Medicare and Medicaid. In the first stage, we use the SIPP data to model program utilization (i.e., use of outpatient services) as a func-

---

[5] Families may receive SSI benefits for a disabled child and Social Security benefits for a surviving child or spouse.

[6] See Duan et al., 1983, for a detailed description of this analytic approach.

tion of educational attainment, age, and individual characteristics. The SIPP does not distinguish between Medicare A and B benefits. However, "Almost all persons entitled to HI [Part A] choose to enroll in SMI [Part B]" (Social Security Administration, July 2004). Because the SIPP does not include institutionalized persons, it does not include Medicaid beneficiaries in long-term care.

In the second stage, for those who have used either program, we model hospitalization (i.e., use of inpatient services) as a function of education level, age, and individual characteristics.

The SIPP does not indicate the amount of Medicare or Medicaid spending on a respondent. We assume that cost per participant is independent of the participant's education level. We use 2002 average payment per beneficiary for inpatient and outpatient services program benefit data from the Centers for Medicare and Medicaid Services of the U.S. Department of Health and Human Services.

Finally, the SIPP does not provide data on Part B premiums. However, premiums are paid regardless of subsequent program utilization, so there is no reason to believe that reductions in utilization related to increased education will be partially offset by reductions in premiums.

Here, too, we run separate models for men and women.

The limits on participation in social support programs were generally introduced well before 2002, when the SIPP data were collected, so their effects are reflected in the data. Hence, our estimates of program participation implicitly take account of the effects of these limits on program participation.

Finally, an increase in a student's education reduces the likelihood that he or she will participate in social support programs and, consequently, reduces the administrative costs of social support programs. Because these savings are small relative to the savings on payments to participants that result from reductions in participation in social support programs, we do not attempt to estimate the savings on administrative costs that taxpayers realize when increases in education reduce social support program participation.

Incarceration Costs

A person with more education is less likely to be unemployed; everything else constant, an individual with a legitimate job is better able to support him- or herself, is less likely to resort to crime, and, consequently, is less likely to be incarcerated. Also, increased educational attainment raises the wage that the person commands in the labor market. This, in turn, raises the costs of crime for the individual in several ways. Incarceration means lost time and lost wages from legal activities, as well as a severe reduction in employment following the correctional period. Indeed, there is substantial empirical evidence showing that higher wages reduce crime (e.g., Machin and Meghir, 2000; Viscusi, 1986).

Educational attainment reduces the likelihood and average duration of incarceration in prisons and jails. These reductions, in turn, reduce demands on the public treasury to build and operate prisons and jails. We model per-person correctional spending as the product of per-person incarceration expenditure and likelihood of individual incarceration. We use the *Sourcebook of Criminal Justice Statistics, 2003* (Pastore and Maguire, 2005) to compute the per-inmate cost of incarceration. We assume that cost per inmate is independent of an inmate's education level.

For state prisons, we use the 1997 administration of the Survey of Inmates in State and Federal Correctional Facilities (U.S. Department of Justice, Bureau of Justice Statistics, and U.S. Department of Justice, Federal Bureau of Prisons, 2001) to estimate the incarcerated population for each education-age-race/ethnicity-gender combination. We also use the 1997 Current Population Survey to estimate general population counts in each corresponding subgroup. Because the Current Population Survey does not include incarcerated persons, we calculate the probability of incarceration as the number of prisoners in each population category divided by the sum of the general population and the number of prisoners for that category.

We follow the same procedure for county and municipal jails, using the 2002 Survey of Inmates of Local Jails (U.S. Department of Justice, Bureau of Justice Statistics, 2006) and, correspondingly, the 2002 Current Population Survey.

Estimating the Effects of Increased Education

We use the models we developed to project the taxes that individuals with given characteristics and a given level of education would pay, the social program benefits they would receive, and the incarceration costs they would impose in each year of their lives from the age at which they left school through age 79. We assume the school-leaving ages are 16 for high school dropouts, 18 for high school graduates, 20 for students who pursue some college, and 22 for students who earn a bachelor's degree.

We use the federal and state income tax and the payroll tax models to estimate the taxes that an individual with given demographic characteristics and education level would pay in each year of his or her life from school-leaving age to age 79. We then discount the estimates for each year of the individual's life to age 18, using appropriate survival rates for the individual's demographic group to control for the probability that a person will die at any given age. The result is an estimate of the present value at age 18 of the taxes an individual from that demographic group will pay between school-leaving and age 79, given his or her education level. We then compare the results for an individual with a given level of education and characteristics against the corresponding results for an individual with the same characteristics but a higher level of education.

The differences between the two sets of results estimate the effects of increased educational attainment on government revenues over an individual's lifetime, holding his or her characteristics constant.

We use a similar approach to estimate the effects of increased educational attainment on the costs of subsidized housing. We use the model of housing subsidy utilization to estimate the probability that an individual with given demographic characteristics and education level would utilize assisted housing in each year of his or her life from school-leaving age to age 79. Assuming that the unit housing cost per person is constant across education levels and demographic groups, the expected housing subsidy is equal to the likelihood of utilization, as predicted by the model, times the average program cost per person. We then discount the estimates for each year of an individual's life to age 18, using appropriate survival rates. The result is an estimate of the present value at age 18 of the assisted housing benefits that would be paid to an individual from that demographic group between school-leaving and age 79, given his or her education level. We then compare the results for an individual with a given level of education and characteristics against the corresponding results for an individual with the same characteristics but a higher level of education. The differences between the two sets of results estimate the effects of increasing the individual's level of education on the assisted housing benefits paid an individual over his or her lifetime, holding his or her characteristics constant.

For each of the other social support and insurance programs, we use the probit model for that program to estimate the likelihood that an individual with given characteristics and education level will participate in that program in each year of his or her life from school-leaving age to age 79. We then use the model of the annual income the individual will receive from that program if they participate in any given year. We multiply the likelihood that the individual will participate in the program in each year by the estimated benefits that the individual would receive in that year if he or she participated to estimate the expected value of the program benefits paid to the individual in each year. We discount the estimates for each year of an individual's life to age 18, using appropriate survival rates. The result is an estimate of the present value at age 18 of the benefits an individual from that demographic group will receive between school leaving and age 79, given his or her education level. We then compare the results for an individual with a given level of education and characteristics against the corresponding results for an individual with the same characteristics but a higher level of education to estimate the effects of educational attainment on the program's costs over the individual's lifetime, holding his or her characteristics constant.

As noted previously, we model per-person correctional spending as the product of per-person incarceration expenditure and the likelihood of individual incarceration, assuming that the probability of incarceration equals the number of prisoners in each population category divided by the sum of the general population and the number of prisoners for that category. We assume that cost per inmate is independent of an inmate's education level.

In making these estimates, we assume that an individual contributes nothing to government revenues and costs while still in school. For example, controlling for demographics, to estimate the effects of graduating from high school rather than dropping out, we subtract the estimated public revenues and costs generated by a high school dropout from age 16 through age 79 from the corresponding estimates of public revenues and costs generated by a high school graduate from age 16 through age 79, assuming that the high school graduate neither contributed to nor drew upon public budgets at ages 17 and 18.

Income received in the future is worth less than income received now, because income received now can earn interest over time. Accordingly, we consider the current value of the future benefits to increases in education. Because much of the data are for the year 2002, we discount all dollar amounts to their equivalent value in 2002. That is, we calculate the number of 2002 dollars that are equal in value to the future dollars that will result from an increase in educational attainment. We discount future benefits to 2002 at an annual average rate of 3 percent per year. We assume that, on average, people are indifferent between receiving $1.00 at any time or $1.03 one year later.

In calculating the present value of the difference in government revenues and costs associated with an increase in education level, we weight the difference in each year of life by the likelihood that an individual with given age, race/ethnicity, and sex will live to that age (Arias, 2004).

The education variables are jointly significant at the 0.001 level in all the regression models used to estimate the effects of education level on tax payments and payments to social support and insurance programs. See Appendix B for details. The education variables are jointly significant in all social program utilization and income models at the 0.05 level or better, except for welfare income, food stamp income, and Unemployment Insurance income for men; hospitalization for women; and SSI income of men and women over 64. For details, see Appendix C.

Transformations

We used either logarithmic or square-root transformations of the amounts of taxes paid and of social program costs in estimating the models of those amounts. This is customary in analyses of financial variables because the variables are generally right-skewed, as is true in the taxes paid and social program costs we examine here. Only 31 of about 43,000 full-year SIPP observations had declared negative annual income, and none collected negative social program benefits. The large majority of the observations tend to be clustered at a relatively small level, but a few observations are for very large amounts. For example, most families' federal income taxes are less than $5,000, but a very small percentage of families pay more than $50,000 in federal income taxes. The few observations with very large values can dominate the estimation, such that, although the resulting model describes the relationship between the independent variables and the average value of the dependent variable, it does not describe well the relationship between the independent variables and the value of the dependent variable in the typical case. Using logarithmic or square root transformations reduces the influence of the outliers, so that the model more accurately describes the relationships for the large majority of cases.

We compared the differences between the fifth and fiftieth and the fiftieth and ninety-fifth percentiles to decide between the logarithmic and square-root transformations.

When we use the logarithmic transformations to estimate the taxes that individuals with a given level of education and given characteristics will pay or the social program benefits they will obtain in each year of their life, we take antilogarithms of the projected values to convert the estimates to dollars. In doing so, we obtain projections of the median values of the taxes and benefits. When we use the square-root transformations, we square the projected values to convert the estimates to dollars. The resulting projections are close to the median. In right-skewed distributions such as those examined here, the median is less than the mean. Consequently, our approach generally underestimates the effects of education level on government revenues and costs.

Critical Assumptions

Throughout this analysis, we assume that the relationships we observe in the SIPP data between individuals' education levels and government revenues and costs reflect the effects of educational attainment on earnings and, consequently, on tax payments, participation in and benefits from social support programs, and incarceration. There is powerful evidence that increases in educational attainment result in higher earnings, on average. Higher earnings translate directly into higher tax payments. As noted previously, higher earnings both limit eligibility for participation in most social support programs and are inversely related to the benefits to participants in most social support programs. Hence, it is reasonable to assume that educational attainment is related to social program costs. Finally, there is substantial evidence that higher earnings reduce the likelihood of participation in criminal activities. Nonetheless, we cannot exclude the possibility that the observed relationships between education level and social program costs and incarceration may also reflect the influence of other factors that affect both educational attainment and participation in social programs or in crime.

To explore the extent to which our results are sensitive to the assumption that the observed relationships reflect the effects of education on public revenues and costs, we replicated all the calculations assuming that the effects of increases in education were 25 percent smaller than our estimates.

As noted above, we use data collected in 2002 to estimate the models used in this analysis. In doing so, we assume that the estimated relationships between education level and governmental revenues and costs will remain approximately the same into the future. Specifically, we assume that the effects of education on income and, consequently, on tax payments, participation in social programs, and incarceration in the future will be generally the same as the effects observed in 2002. We also assume that federal, state, and local tax structures, social support programs, and incarceration patterns will not change substantially in the future.

The level of education needed to succeed in labor markets has been increasing for decades. And the earnings gaps between individuals with differing levels of education have consequently grown consistently over time. It seems likely that the gaps that existed in 2002 when the data used to estimate our models were collected will, if anything, widen into the future. If they do so, the effects of education level on government revenues and costs will exceed the estimates presented here. If the increases in relative income resulting from increases in education level grow over time, they will cause greater increases in relative tax payments and greater decreases in participation in social programs and in incarceration.

Federal and state tax structures are changed from time to time, but the changes are generally marginal. Tax brackets and rates are occasionally modified, and deductions are introduced or eliminated. The Economic Recovery Act of 1981 shifted some of the federal tax burden from individuals to businesses, effectively shifting the federal tax more toward a consumption tax. The Taxpayer Relief Act of 1997 introduced tax credits, in essence a spending program operating through the tax system. But the overall structure has not been significantly changed for decades.

Similarly, the rates and ceilings that determine Social Security and Medicare contributions have been increased over time, but the general structure of the systems remain the same. If anything, the growing federal budget deficit and growing concerns for the future of the Social Security and Medicare systems as baby boomers begin to hit retirement suggest that the payroll taxes levied to support these programs will increase over time. If that occurs, the estimates presented here will understate the effects of increased educational attainment on contributions to government revenues.

Recent legislation has introduced disincentives for participation in social programs. Commonly called "welfare reform," the 1996 Personal Responsibility and Work Opportunity Reconciliation Act and the 1997 Balanced Budget Act have resulted in more stringent eligibility rules for many programs and in lifetime-total and one-time caps on participation in income support programs. There has not been significant debate over the structure of these programs since then.

It is obviously possible that the structure of one or more of the social programs we consider here will be significantly modified sometime in the future. The 1996 and

1997 changes generally reflected concerns that these programs were too often used by people who did not need the support offered by the programs. This suggests that future changes, if any, are more likely to further reduce access to these programs. If so, increases in the income differential associated with increases in education will result in greater reductions in social program participation and, consequently, greater costs than the estimates presented here.

Incarceration patterns reflect both criminal activity and sentencing patterns. Changes in sentencing guidelines and in early release programs stimulated by prison or jail overcrowding will influence incarceration patterns and, consequently, costs. We are not aware of any systematic trends in the factors that affect incarceration costs. Therefore, the patterns and costs implied by the available data are the best available basis for the estimates.

Putting the Results in Perspective

In this study, we estimate the effects of increased educational attainment on three major types of government revenues and costs that directly affect taxpayers and for which data are available. These types of revenues and costs are

- increased tax payments and payments into social support and insurance programs
- reduced spending on social support and insurance programs
- reduced spending on prisons and jails.

Our estimates are based on models developed using the 2002 SIPP data. The models themselves are subject to statistical variation. If a somewhat different set of individuals had been included in the SIPP survey, the data would be slightly different and the resulting models somewhat different.

However, the statistical variation in the models pales in comparison to the uncertainty inherent in estimating future trends and patterns. As noted above, our specific estimates are based on several fundamental assumptions. We assume that the relationships between education level and income and the consequent relationships between education level and tax payments, social program participation and benefits, and incarceration patterns will not change significantly over time.

Changes in some of these relationships are likely to occur at some future date. Consequently, the estimates presented here cannot be viewed as precise. However, as we will demonstrate in subsequent sections of this report, the magnitudes of the estimates are generally so large that even changes that substantially reduce the effects of increases in educational attainment on government revenues and costs will not reduce the effects of such increases to zero. Moreover, changes that increase the effects of educational attainment on government revenues and costs are more likely than are changes that reduce such effects. If such changes occur, the estimates presented here will understate the effects of educational attainment on government revenues and costs.

Our analysis assumes that the relationships observed in the data are causal. That is, we assume that the differences in contributions to government revenues and costs between more highly educated and less highly educated people are the result of the differences in their levels of education. There is abundant evidence that increased educational attainment leads to increases in earnings and that earnings are related to contributions to government revenues and costs. It is possible that some other factor is related to both the level of an individual's education and his or her contributions to government revenues and costs. But it is clear that education is a dominant factor, even if there are others. Moreover, the magnitude of the effect of education on earnings has grown consistently over time. Because we assume that the relationships between education and contributions to government revenues and costs that existed in 2002 will continue over time, our estimates do not reflect the effects of increases in the effect of education on earnings and, consequently, on government revenues and costs.

The bottom line is that the analyses that follow, notwithstanding the inherent uncertainties in estimating future trends and patterns, show that increases in educational attainment yield significant benefits to taxpayers. We recognize that the greatest gains accrue to those whose education levels are improved and that increases in educational attainment also provide numerous types of noneconomic benefits in addition to economic benefits. However, this analysis indicates that raising an individual's level of education creates high benefits for the public budget, benefits that should be considered in assessing the importance of finding, funding, and implementing programs for increasing education levels.

CHAPTER THREE

Payments for Taxes and Social Programs

Greater educational attainment increases both the likelihood of employment and an individual's earnings when employed. The higher income realized by more highly educated people results in higher federal and state income taxes. "Consumption" taxes, such as sales, real estate, and excise taxes, also increase as a direct result of higher income. Taxes on consumption and property depend on the amounts spent on consumption and property, which, in turn, depend on individual and household disposable income. Therefore, as a by-product of earning higher incomes, people with more schooling generally pay more in taxes.

In addition, the higher earnings realized by more highly educated people results in higher payments to social support and insurance programs, such as Social Security and Medicare. Payments to social support and insurance programs by individuals and their employers are determined by earnings. So, as a by-product of higher earnings, people with more schooling and their employers generally pay more to social support and insurance programs.

In this chapter, we review the relevant taxation mechanisms that determine tax payments and payments to social support and insurance programs and present the results of our analysis of the effects of educational attainment on payments into the public budget.

Appendix B presents the empirical analyses used to estimate the effects of increased educational attainment on tax payments and payments to social support and insurance programs.[1]

Taxation Mechanisms

Individuals and households contribute to the public budget by paying taxes. In this study we concentrate on three types of tax payments:

---

[1] The education variables are jointly significant at the 0.001 level in all the regression models used to estimate the effects of education level on tax payments and payments to social support and insurance programs. See Appendix B for details.

Federal personal income taxes—taxes on income levied at the federal level. We use family income data from the 2002 administrations of the SIPP (U.S. Census Bureau, 2005a, 2005b, 2005c) and 2002 taxation rates by income group (Parisi, 2004–2005) to estimate federal income tax payment on a family basis. We split this amount among all adults in the family to compute tax payments by individuals. We then model payments as a function of education level, age, and demographic characteristics (gender, place of birth, and race/ethnicity). Finally, we forecast payments throughout the entire life of an adult through age 79 using appropriate survival rates to estimate the differential impact of education level on public revenues.

This approach understates the effects of education on federal income tax payments. Because more highly educated people earn more, on average, and federal income taxes are progressive, the more highly educated adults in a family contribute disproportionately more to the family's tax obligation. By attributing a proportional share of federal tax payments to each adult in the family, we understate the effects of education level on federal tax payments.

We excluded Earned Income Tax Credits (EITCs) due to highly inadequate data in the SIPP. In the full SIPP topical tax module sample of 68,700 people, 66,800 did not even answer the EITC question. Another 900 responded "don't know." Only 862 claimed any EITC. Response choices for EITC amount were in terms of brackets of $200, and 122 of the responses (15 percent of the beneficiary subsample) were in the broad "more than $3,500" category.

EITC is now the largest transfer program, larger than Temporary Assistance to Needy Families. Because increases in education level result in higher earnings, increases in education level will reduce the likelihood of participation in EITC. The exclusion of EITC from this analysis therefore biases the estimates of the effects of education on the costs of social support programs downward.

Federal payroll taxes—taxes on earnings levied at the federal level that finance Social Security and Medicare benefits. We use individual earnings data from the 2002 administrations of the SIPP and statutory tax rates (and the Social Security tax cap) to estimate payroll tax payment on individual basis. However, payroll taxes are paid only by those who have any earnings. Therefore, we first model the probability of employment as a function of education level, age, and demographic characteristics. For those individuals who work, we then model tax payments based on educational attainment, age, and demographic characteristics. Finally, we forecast payments throughout the entire life of an adult through age 79, using appropriate survival rates, to estimate with the differential impact of education level on public revenues.

State income, property, and sales taxes—taxes on income that are levied at the state level and taxes on consumption that are levied at the state and local level, including sales, real estate, and excise taxes. We use family income data from the 2002 administrations of the SIPP and national average state and local tax rates by income group to estimate state tax payments on a family basis. We divide this amount evenly among the adults in the household to compute average tax payments by individuals. We then model payments as a function of education level, age, and demographic characteristics. Finally, we forecast payments throughout the entire working life of an adult to calculate the differential impact of education level on public revenues.

This approach underestimates the effects of increases in education on state tax payments. When a family includes two or more adults, we assume the tax payments made by the family are evenly distributed among the adults. Accordingly, we understate the contributions the higher-paid members of the family contribute to the family's tax payments and overstate the contributions lower-paid members of the family contribute to the family's tax payments. Because more highly educated people are generally the more highly paid members of a family, we underestimate the effects of an individual's education level on his or her contributions to state tax payments.

Appendix B provides the details of the models we used to estimate the effects of education level on state tax payments.

Educational Attainment and Earnings

Educational attainment increases the likelihood of being employed and it increases wages when employed. More education also increases the likelihood of labor force participation, so the effects of education level on income are greater than the effects on earnings alone.

The distributions of both annual average individual earnings and annual average family income in our data exhibit a strong association with education level, as can be seen in Tables 3.1a and 3.1b. For a sample of roughly 40,000 nationally representative individuals covered in all months of 2002 by the SIPP, the summary figures indicate that both average individual income and average family incomes rise steeply with education level.

Table 3.1a shows the average earnings by education level and ethnicity for all persons in the sample, including those not employed. Accordingly, they reflect the effects of education on both employed persons' wages and salaries and the likelihood that a person will be employed and, if employed, their hours worked. For the entire sample, bachelor's degree holders, on average, earn more than two times what high school graduates earn. For Asians this ratio rises to three times. Comparable differences are not as large for family incomes, probably as a result of congregation of high earners and low earners within households.

Table 3.1b shows average family income. The data include only cash income. In-kind benefits, such as food stamps or Medicaid benefits, are not included.

Table 3.1a
Average 2002 Individual Annual Earnings, by Ethnicity and Education Level

Education Level	White	Asian	Black	Hispanic	All
Bachelor's degree or more	42,155	44,082	33,282	36,504	41,491
Some college	22,249	18,537	19,031	21,436	21,728
High school graduate	16,662	14,389	13,475	15,862	16,125
Less than high school graduate	7,549	7,902	4,968	10,090	7,847
All	24,097	26,468	15,446	16,366	22,379

SOURCE: Survey of Income and Program Participation 2002 Panel, 2005.

Table 3.1b
Average 2002 Family Annual Income, by Ethnicity and Education Level

Highest Education Level in Family	White	Asian	Black	Hispanic	All
Bachelor's degree or more	84,424	87,886	67,291	76,504	83,251
Some college	59,335	59,797	44,163	54,518	57,348
High school graduate	49,172	50,661	35,863	42,795	46,923
Less than high school graduate	33,159	42,033	23,369	33,900	31,994
All	59,814	66,688	39,095	44,387	56,070

SOURCE: Survey of Income and Program Participation 2002 Panel, 2005.

Federal and State Tax Rates

Individuals and households contribute to the public budget by paying taxes. In this study, we concentrate on federal personal income taxes, federal payroll taxes, and state income, property, and sales taxes.

Federal Income Tax Rates

The federal income tax, paid to the Internal Revenue Service, is progressive; that is, the share of a person's income paid in federal income taxes increases with income, and, consequently, education level, at an increasing rate. Table 3.2 illustrates the progressive nature of the federal income tax. It shows the average tax rate paid by income level in 2002. For example, while those with income between $30,000 and $50,000 pay 8 percent of their income in federal income taxes, on average, those with incomes between $100,000 and $200,000 pay almost twice that percentage. Thus, the public benefits of increased educational attainment occur on an accelerated basis as far as federal income taxes are concerned.

Table 3.2
Average Federal Income Tax Rates and Related Data, by Income

Adjusted Gross Income ($)	Average Tax Rate (%)	Adjusted Gross Income ($, millions)	Amount of Benefits ($, thousands)	Average Adjusted Gross Income ($)
All	14.1	5,641,128	90,964	62,015
Under $10,000	2.5	36,492	5,316	6,865
$10,000–$20,000	4.6	198,171	13,089	15,140
$20,000–$30,000	6.7	321,667	12,877	24,980
$30,000–$50,000	8.0	883,965	22,482	39,319
$50,000–$100,000	10.6	1,844,319	26,377	69,921
$100,000–$200,000	15.8	1,107,803	8,408	131,756
$200,000–$500,000	22.8	548,162	1,906	287,598
$500,000–$1,000,000	27.9	226,745	336	674,836
Over $1,000,000	28.6	474,933	169	2,810,254

SOURCE: Parisi (2004–2005, Figure B).

Payroll Tax Rates

Individuals pay Social Security and Medicare taxes out of personal income based on legally imposed payroll tax rates (Table 3.3). Social Security taxes finance the Old-Age and Survivors Insurance and the Disability Insurance programs. Medicare taxes finance the Hospital Insurance part of Medicare. The employer and employee each pay a tax equal to 5.3 percent of the employee's income for Old-Age and Survivors Insurance, 0.9 percent for Disability Insurance, and 1.45 percent for Hospital Insurance, for a total of 15.3 percent (Social Security Administration, 2005). For Social Security contributions, taxable earnings are capped at a level that is adjusted each year according to national average wage. That ceiling was $84,900 in 2002 (Social Security Administration, 2002). Since 1993, a total Medicare tax of 2.9 percent has been applied to all earnings.

Table 3.3
Statutory 2002 Payroll Tax Rates and Medicare Tax Cap

	Rate (%)	Ceiling ($)	Maximum Tax ($)
Old-Age and Survivors Insurance	10.6	84,900	8,999
Disability Insurance	1.8	84,900	1,528
Subtotal, Social Security	12.4	84,900	10,528
Medicare (Hospital Insurance)	2.9	–	–
Total	15.3	–	–

SOURCES: Social Security Administration (2002, 2005).

Average State Tax Rates

Individuals and families also contribute to the budgets of state and local governments. Such contributions include personal and corporate income taxes, property taxes, and sales and excise taxes. While many of these are levied on current (e.g., sales tax) or accumulated (e.g., property tax) consumption, in effect they are proportional to personal and family income. For state and local taxes, we use national average taxation rates for the United States as computed and reported by the Institute on Taxation and Economic Policy (McIntyre et al., 2003). Table 3.4 shows the total of state and local taxes in the United States (after the federal offset).

The Effects of Increased Educational Attainment on Tax Payments

Increased educational attainment is rewarded in the job market with a higher likelihood of being employed and higher income when employed. The government carves out a proportion of the private benefits to education; i.e., from the individual who earned more as a result of his increased education, both directly via income taxes and indirectly via payroll and consumption taxes. We estimated the increase in the 2002 value of what an individual would contribute in taxes if he or she were to increase his or her education from one level to the next level—from high school dropout to high school graduation, from high school graduation to some college, and from some college to college graduation.[2]

Table 3.4
State and Local Tax Rates for 2002, U.S. Average

Income Group	1st 20%	2nd 20%	Mid 20%	4th 20%	Next 15%	Next 4%	Top 1%
Upper limit ($ thousands)	16	26	42	72	154	318	–
Average income ($ thousands)	10	21	33	55	100	211	1,129
Sales and excise taxes (%)	7.8	6.4	5.1	4.1	3.1	2.0	1.1
Property taxes (%)	3.1	2.3	2.5	2.6	2.6	2.3	1.4
Income taxes (%)	0.6	1.6	2.3	2.7	3.2	3.8	4.8
Total taxes (%)	11.4	10.4	9.9	9.4	8.9	8.1	7.3
Federal deduction offset (%)	0	–0.1	–0.3	–0.6	–1.2	–1.6	–2.0
Total after offset (%)	11.4	10.3	9.6	8.8	7.7	6.5	5.2

SOURCE: McIntyre et al. (2003).
NOTE: 2000 dollars in original adjusted to 2002 using the Consumer Price Index.

---

[2] Appendix B presents the empirical analyses used to estimate the effects of increasing education on tax payments and payments to social support and insurance programs.

Figure 3.1 shows the discounted present value, in 2002 dollars, of the additional tax payments a native-born man, by race/ethnic group, would pay over his lifetime, on average, if he increased his education level.

The present value of the additional taxes a native-born white man who graduates from high school would pay over his lifetime would be about $54,000 greater than the present value of the taxes he would pay had he dropped out of high school. If a U.S.-born white man goes on to college, but does not graduate, the present value of his tax payments over his lifetime will be about $37,000 more than if he had not continued his education beyond high school. If a native-born white man graduates from college, the 2002 value of his tax payments would increase substantially—about $120,000—above what he would pay in taxes if he had some college, but did graduate. As the chart illustrates, the findings are similar for native-born men in other race/ethnic groups.

Figure 3.2 shows the average effect of increased educational attainment (relative to a high school dropout) on the present value, in 2002 dollars, of lifetime tax payments by a native-born woman by race/ethnic group.

For a native-born white woman, graduating from high school increases the 2002 value of tax payment about $50,000, completing some college further increases the 2002 value of tax payment about $42,000, and graduating from college further

Figure 3.1
Present Value of Lifetime Increases in Tax Payments Resulting from Increased Education, U.S.-Born Men

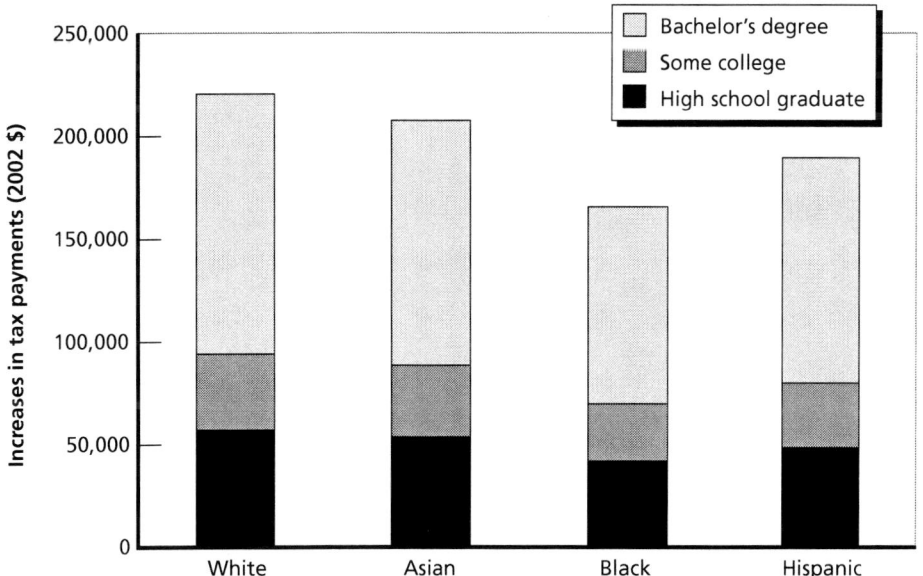

NOTES: The figure shows increases relative to the average taxes paid by a high school dropout. Dollar amounts are expressed in 2002 dollars discounted to age 18 using a 3 percent real discount rate.

RAND MG686-3.1

Figure 3.2
Present Value of Lifetime Increases in Tax Payments Resulting from Increased Educational Attainment, U.S.-Born Women

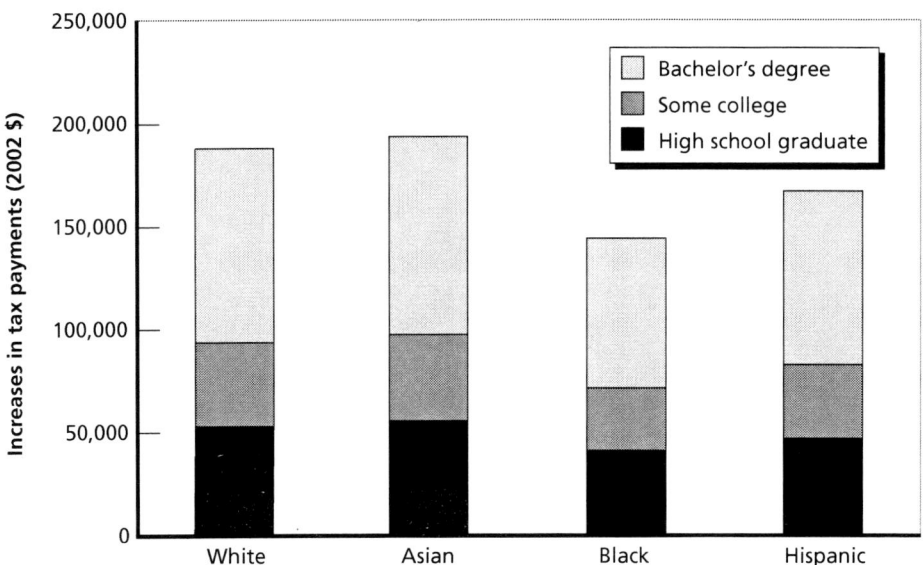

NOTES: The figure shows increases relative to the average taxes paid by a high school dropout. Dollar amounts are expressed in 2002 dollars discounted to age 18 using a 3 percent real discount rate.
RAND MG686-3.2

increases the 2002 value of tax payment about $90,000. The findings are similar for native-born women in other race/ethnic groups.

Related Studies

The estimates are roughly equivalent to those obtained by Belfield and Levin (2007) and by Rouse (2005). Belfield and Levin found that, assuming a 3.5 percent discount rate and a 1.5 percent rate of productivity growth, the present value, in 2002 dollars,[3] of the effect of increasing a student's education from high school dropout to high school graduate or more, on his or her federal, state, and local tax payments would range from $41,000 (black woman) to $153,000 (white man), depending on gender and race/ethnicity. Over all demographic groups, the average effect of an increase in education from high school dropout to high school graduate or more is about $85,000, present value, in 2002 dollars.

---

[3] Belfield and Levin present their results in the present value in 2007 of the effects of the increase in education. We discounted their estimates to 2002 to compare them with our estimates.

Rouse estimated that, assuming a 3.5 percent discount rate and 0 percent productivity growth, the discounted present value of the additional federal, state, and local taxes paid by a high school graduate compared with a high school dropout is about $65,000 in 2002 dollars.[4] She estimated that the discounted present value of the increase in taxes paid by a high school graduate or more compared to a high school dropout is about $145,000 in 2002 dollars.

The Effects of Multilevel Increases in Educational Attainment on Tax Payments

The effects of multilevel increases in an individual's education on the 2002 value of tax payments will be somewhat smaller than the sum of the effects of increasing education from one level to the next for the relevant levels. The estimates of the effects of increasing education from one level to the next reported above assume income and, therefore, tax payments, increase as soon as the next level is reached. However, when an individual moves up two or three levels, the benefits from the initial increase are not realized until the individual has moved through the second, or third, level.

Table 3.5 lists the estimated increase in the 2002 value of what an individual would contribute in taxes if he or she graduated from college instead of dropping out of high school. A white native-born man who completes college rather than dropping out of high school would pay about $192,000 more in taxes and contributions to social insurance over his lifetime as a result of his additional schooling. This is less than the sum of the estimates in the first column of Figure 3.1. The estimated increase in the 2002 value of tax payments for increasing education from less than high school to high school graduate shown in Figure 3.1 assumes that the high school graduate begins earning income, and paying taxes, on completion of high school. The estimated increase in the 2002 value of tax payments for increasing education from less than high school to college graduate shown in Table 3.5 assumes the individual not only completes high school, but goes on to complete college and, consequently, defers earning income and paying taxes for four more years.

Sensitivity Analysis

To explore the extent to which our results are sensitive to the estimates of the effects of education level on tax payments, we replicated all the calculations assuming that the effects of increases in educational attainment were 25 percent smaller than our

---

[4] Rouse presents her results in the present value in 2004 of the effects of the increase in education. We discounted her estimates to 2002 to compare them with our estimates.

Table 3.5
Increased Tax Payments Associated with Increasing Educational Attainment from High School Dropout to College Graduate, U.S.-Born Men and Women

Race/Ethnicity	Increased Tax Payments (2002 $, thousands)	
	Men	Women
White	192	167
Asian	181	171
Black	144	128
Hispanic	165	148

SOURCE: Appendix B.

estimates. We then calculated the percentage reduction in the estimated effect of an increase in education level for each of the native-born populations if the effect of the increase in education on tax payments were only 75 percent of our estimate. Table 3.6 shows the range of percentage reductions across the native-born demographic groups for each increase in the level of education. It also shows the native-born demographic group for which each percentage reduction was observed.

For example, we replicated all the calculations assuming that the effects of increases in education from less than high school graduate to high school graduate on tax payments were 25 percent smaller than our estimates. The revised estimates for the native-born demographic groups were 21 percent (white women) to 23 percent (Hispanic men) lower than the original estimates. In sum, even if we overestimated the effects of education level on the present value of tax payments by 25 percent, increases in educational attainment still result in substantial increases in the present value of tax payments.

Reducing the estimate of the effect of an increase in education level on tax payments has essentially the same result for all demographic groups. The range of percent-

Table 3.6
Range of Percentage Reduction in Tax Payments If the Effect of Increased Education Is Reduced 25 Percent, U.S.-Born Men and Women

Increase in Education Level	Percentage Reduction
Less than high school graduate to high school graduate	21 (white woman) to 23 (Hispanic man)
High school graduate to some college	27 (Hispanic man) to 27 (Asian woman)
Some college to bachelor's degree or more	31 (Hispanic man) to 32 (Asian woman)
Less than high school graduate to bachelor's degree or more	28 (black woman) to 28 (Asian woman)

age reductions in tax payments across the groups is generally narrow. Reducing the estimated effect of increased educational attainment generally has a smaller effect on the tax payment estimates for increasing education from less than high school graduate to high school graduate than on the estimates for the other increases in education level.

Table 3.7 shows the smallest estimated increase in tax payments resulting from an increase in education level across the native-born demographic groups if the estimate of the effects of the increase in education is reduced 25 percent. For example, suppose we assume that our estimate of the effect of increasing education from less than high school graduate to high school graduate on tax payments is 25 percent too high. If we recalculate the effect on tax payments assuming the education effects are 75 percent of our estimates, the lowest estimate of the present value in 2002 dollars of the increase in tax payments that would result from that increase in education from less than high school graduate to high school graduate among native-born groups is about $30,000 for a black man. The estimated increase in tax payments for each of the other seven demographic groups, assuming that the effect of increasing education from less than high school graduate to high school graduate is only 75 percent as large as our estimate, is larger.

The results presented in Table 3.7 show that, even if our estimates of the effects of education on tax payments are substantially too high, increased educational attainment still results in substantial benefits to taxpayers in the form of increased tax payments by those whose education is increased.

Summary

Our results show that increases in the education level of individuals in every population subgroup result in a substantial increase in tax payments. Earning a bachelor's

Table 3.7
Smallest Estimated Effect of Increased Education on Tax Payments If Effect of Increased Education Is Reduced 25 Percent, U.S.-Born Men and Women

Increase in Education Level	Smallest Estimated Increase in Tax Payments (2002 $, thousands)
Less than high school graduate to high school graduate	30 (black man)
High school graduate to some college	20 (black man)
Some college to bachelor's degree or more	47 (black woman)
Less than high school graduate to bachelor's degree or more	92 (black woman)

degree or more rather than completing only some college has the largest impact on tax payments, followed by graduating high school rather than dropping out, and finally completing some college rather than only graduating high school.

The estimates presented for both single-level increments in education (Figures 3.1 and 3.2) and multilevel increments (Table 3.5) clearly indicate that increases in the education level of individuals in every population subgroup result in substantial benefits to taxpayers, due to increases in the present value of the increased tax payments that result from increases in education.

CHAPTER FOUR
Spending on Social Support Programs

The United States has built an extensive safety net for the poor and needy. Increases in educational attainment result in increases in earnings that, in turn, result in a reduced likelihood that a person will draw on this safety net and a decrease in the amount of benefit a person will receive from most social programs if he or she participates. In this chapter, we estimate the effects of increased educational attainment on social support program spending in each of the eight largest social support and insurance programs for which sufficient data on program participation and spending are available.

Appendix C presents the empirical analyses used to estimate the effects of increased educational attainment on participation in social programs and the resulting costs.[1]

Background

The U.S. social support and insurance system includes some 400 programs in two dozen federal departments and agencies. Some programs are administered jointly by the federal and state governments. Social support programs can be broadly divided into two categories.

The first category consists of social support programs that provide cash and noncash benefits to members of low-income households in programs that provide direct income support, medical support, food and nutrition, and housing. Major programs of this type include the Temporary Assistance for Needy Families, Earned Income Tax Credit, housing subsidies, the Supplemental Nutrition Assistance Program (food stamps), SSI, and Medicaid.

The second category consists of social insurance programs that replace the lost income of people who cannot work because of old age, disability, severance, etc. Major programs of this type include Medicare, Unemployment Insurance, and Social Secu-

---

[1] The education variables are jointly significant in all social program utilization and income models at the 0.05 level or better, except for welfare income, food stamp income, and Unemployment Insurance income of men; hospitalization of women; and SSI income of men and women over 64. For details, see Appendix C.

rity. Laws passed in the 1990s have reduced the federal burden and introduced disincentives for program participation for some means-tested programs. Commonly called "welfare reform," the 1996 Personal Responsibility and Work Opportunity Reconciliation Act and the 1997 Balanced Budget Act have resulted in a number of changes:

- a shifting of more responsibility to state governments
- revision of eligibility rules for many programs
- lifetime-total and one-time caps on participation in income support programs
- replacement of some old programs with new ones (for example, Aid to Families with Dependent Children was replaced with the Temporary Assistance to Needy Families and the Child Care Development Fund)
- the launching of new programs (for example, the State Children's Health Insurance Fund, which is basically Medicaid for children).

Among the hundreds of social support and insurance programs, a handful account for half of total social program spending, and about a dozen make up 90 percent of the total. We examine the largest social support and insurance programs for which sufficient data on program participation and program spending are available. These include the following:

- welfare programs (Temporary Assistance to Needy Families, general assistance, and other welfare)
- subsidized housing (public housing and rental assistance)
- food stamps (the Supplemental Nutrition Assistance Program)
- SSI
- Medicaid
- Medicare
- Unemployment Insurance
- Social Security (retirement, disability, and survivor programs).

Analytic Approach

There is little research that explicitly explores the link between social programs and educational attainment. In a review of factors that affect dependence on social support and insurance programs, Moffitt (1992) notes that studies controlling for education level find higher participation rates for people with lower educational attainment. Also, when program utilization is examined over time, exit rates are higher for people with higher levels of education (or higher wages, which is a causal product of more education). Krop et al. (2000) demonstrate a link between educational attainment and expected public savings for a range of social support and insurance programs.

As discussed in Chapter Two, greater educational attainment leads to better opportunities in the job market. Higher levels of education result in both higher likelihood of employment and higher earnings when employed. The decision to participate in a social support program is dictated by a comparison of the benefits available from that program and the earnings forgone in the labor market. The more educated the individual, the more he or she can command in the labor market. Therefore, increased education makes social support program participation less attractive. Moreover, most social support programs have stringent participation criteria related to current income or assets. Anything that improves a person's earnings potential reduces his or her participation in social support programs. Further, the benefits provided to participants in most social support programs are inversely related to the participant's income. Higher earning participants receive lower benefits in most social support programs.

The converse is true for most social insurance programs. Eligibility for some social insurance programs depends on having been employed for some period of time, and the amount of benefits provided to a beneficiary sometimes depend on the amounts paid into the program by the beneficiary or on behalf of the beneficiary. Because more highly educated individuals are more likely to be employed and likely to earn more when employed, more highly educated people are more likely to qualify for social insurance and likely to receive higher benefits when they draw on the program.

Program utilization and benefits are a function of income and individual attributes, including education level. But again, education level directly affects earnings and, consequently, directly affects both participation in welfare programs and the amount received when participating. Accordingly, we develop two types of reduced form models: those that estimate the relationship between program *participation* and education level and other personal characteristics, and those that estimate the relationship between program *benefits* and education and other personal characteristics

We obtained program participation data from the 2002 SIPP for the eight programs we consider. The SIPP also provides data on the amount of benefit received by the individual or family for welfare, food stamps, Unemployment Insurance, SSI, and Social Security. In each of these programs, we use a two-part model to assess the effect of educational attainment on program benefits. In the first stage, we model program utilization as a function of educational attainment, age, gender, race/ethnicity, and place of birth. In the second stage, for those who are program participants, we model annual income from the particular program as a function of educational attainment, age, gender, race/ethnicity, and place of birth. Finally, we combine results from both models to derive program benefits by education level.

For Medicare and Medicaid, we use 2002 utilization data from the SIPP and 2002 program benefit data from the Centers for Medicare and Medicaid Services of the U.S. Department of Health and Human Services. Because these data are not stratified by education or any other variable we're interested in, we assume that that Medicare and Medicaid cost per user is constant across education levels and demographic groups. We use average payment per beneficiary or service user for inpatient and outpatient services (Table 4.1). We again use a two-part model for each program. In the first stage, we use the SIPP data to model program utilization (i.e., use of outpatient services) as a function of educational attainment, age, and other demographic characteristics. In the second stage, for those who have used either program, we model hospitalization (i.e., use of inpatient services) as a function of education level, age, and other variables.

For subsidized housing, we use HUD data on total annual program cost and number of residents covered. We assume that unit housing cost per person is constant across education levels and demographic groups. This makes a single-part model, in which housing-subsidy utilization depends on education level, age, and other variables, sufficient. Then, the expected housing subsidy is equal to the likelihood of utilization, as predicted by the single-part model, times the average program cost per person.

Three of the programs—SSI, Social Security, and Medicare—each include two components, one addressed to the disabled and the other to the elderly. Accordingly, we conducted separate analyses for younger and older subpopulations in analyzing the effects of educational attainment on program benefits.

Findings related to each social program are provided below, along with a brief description of each of the programs. To illustrate the results, we show the effects of increased educational attainment on social program costs for U.S.-born Hispanic women. The details of our analyses of these programs are provided in Appendix C. It describes the data sources, economic models, and the empirical estimations. It also discusses some caveats related to the research methods.

Effects of Educational Attainment on the Costs of Welfare Programs

For the purposes of this study, "welfare programs" include Temporary Assistance to Needy Families, general assistance, and other similar assistance programs for the needy.

Table 4.1
Medicare and Medicaid Benefit Estimates, 2002

	Payments ($ billion)	Beneficiaries ($ million)	Benefit per Beneficiary ($)
Medicare			
Inpatient	123.0	7.8	15,694
Outpatient	92.4	31.5	2,934
Medicaid			
Inpatient	57.5	5.0	11,401
Outpatient	49.1	24.4	2,016

NOTE: Medicare data use calendar year; Medicaid data use fiscal year.
SOURCE: U.S. Department of Health and Human Services, Centers for Medicare and Medicaid Services (2006).

We considered these programs as one unit in our analysis, since they have similar criteria for participation and pay out smaller amounts compared with other social support and insurance programs analyzed in the study.

Fewer than 2 percent of the individuals in the nationally representative SIPP data received welfare program benefits, making it the least utilized of the social support programs we studied. For beneficiaries, welfare income in 2002 averaged $2,200 per year, with a high of $11,700.

The results show that the largest public saving in welfare programs would come from high school dropouts who stayed in school and became high school graduates. This is true for all groups, regardless of gender, race/ethnicity, and place of birth. Benefits paid to female high school dropouts are ten times those paid to male high school dropouts. This gap is primarily driven by the huge welfare program participation gap between the genders, which reflects program design features: Most two-parent families do not qualify, and most single-parent families that do qualify are headed by women. The highest participation rates are 25 percent, for 18-year-old black women who lack a high school diploma, and 17 percent, for their Hispanic counterparts.

Savings peak for women when they are in their late twenties—prime child-bearing age—and in the late forties for men. Figure 4.1 illustrates the savings for women, using a U.S.-born Hispanic woman as an example.

If the woman in our example dropped out of high school, she would receive a little over $300 per year in welfare benefits when she is age 20. The top, solid line shows

Figure 4.1
Expected Annual Welfare Program Spending for a U.S.-Born Hispanic Woman

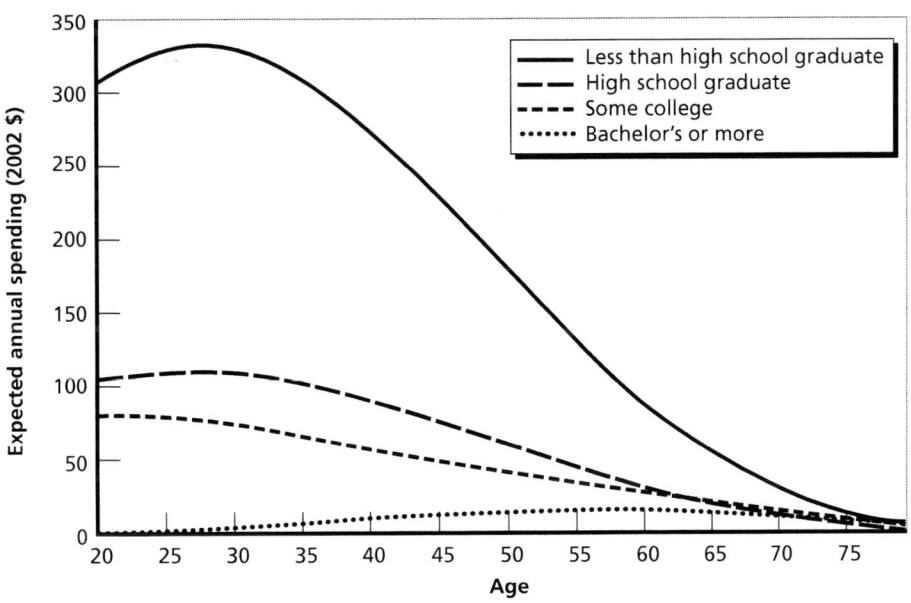

RAND MG686-4.1

how the amount of welfare benefits she receives would change as she ages. They peak when she is in her late twenties and decrease steadily after that.

If the same woman earned a bachelor's degree, at age 20 she would receive no welfare benefits—a savings to the public budget of more than $300. The amount of benefits she receives over her lifetime is represented by the bottom, dotted line on the chart.

If the same woman in our example graduated from high school or attended some college, her welfare benefits over the course of her lifetime would begin at around $100 per year at age 20, hold nearly steady for several years, and decline in middle age.

The most dramatic finding illustrated by the chart is that a Hispanic woman who earns at least a high school diploma receives far less in welfare benefits over the course of her lifetime than she would if she dropped out of high school. In addition, the difference between high school graduation and dropping out is more dramatic than the differences between any other of the levels of education in our study. This is true for all groups, regardless of gender, race/ethnicity, and place of birth.

Effects of Educational Attainment on the Costs of Housing Subsidies

HUD maintains a public housing program through which it provides rental housing to low-income families at low cost. In addition, HUD administers the Section 8 Rental Voucher Program, which is intended to help very low-income families obtain decent and safe rental housing. Eligibility for both of these programs relates to income level and lack of available low-cost housing.

We consider the two programs—the public housing program and Section 8 Rental Voucher program—together in our analysis because they have similar criteria for participation and come from the budget of the same federal department. According to the SIPP data, 4 percent of individuals in 2002 resided in public housing, 2 percent received rental assistance, and slightly less than 1 percent used both benefits. According to our analysis of HUD data for 2002, per-resident cost of public housing and Section 8 programs averaged $2,233 per year.

The results show that the largest public saving in subsidized housing occurs between high school dropouts and high school graduates, across all gender, race/ethnicity, and place-of-birth groups. Figure 4.2 illustrates the results. It shows the difference in the costs of annual public housing subsidies for a U.S-born Hispanic woman as a function of her age and education level.

The savings in spending on housing for women who attain a higher level of education are higher than for men, but by a margin of 50–100 percent, a much more modest difference compared with the differences between men and women in most other social support programs. The cost of a unit of housing is assumed to be the same for men and women, so it may be that this difference is due to the fact that women use

Figure 4.2
Expected Annual Public Housing Subsidies for a U.S.-Born Hispanic Woman

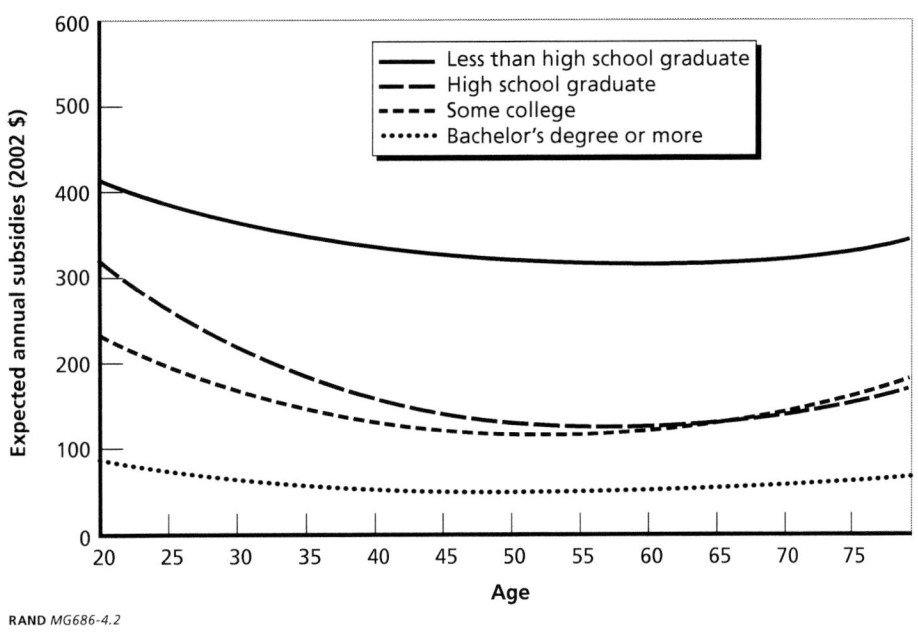

housing subsidies more than men do. On the other hand, it is possible that the difference is due to the fact that most women who receive housing subsidies have children, so they would need a higher subsidy per household than childless men, who can live in smaller units.

The highest savings on housing subsidies would come from U.S.-born black women. Raising their level of education from high school dropout to college graduate would result in savings of $530–$540 per year. On the other hand, U.S.-born white men who graduated from college rather than dropping out of high school would produce a maximum savings of only $100 per year. Savings for both women and men peak twice at the high and low ends of the age spectrum and bottom out at ages 45–50.

Effects of Educational Attainment on the Costs of Food Stamps

The federal food stamp program, renamed the Supplemental Nutrition Assistance Program in 2008, provides benefits to low-income people for purchasing food and improving their diets. Benefits are provided in the form of paper coupons or debit card balances, which can be spent at authorized retail locations. Eligibility criteria relate to current bank balances, annual household income, and responsibility for at least one other person.

Six percent of the individuals in the SIPP data received food stamps. For recipients, the extra income provided by food stamps in 2002 averaged $1,450 per year, with a high of $9,250.

Our results show that the largest public saving in food stamps would result from raising educational attainment from high school dropout to high school graduate, for all gender, race/ethnicity, and place-of-birth groups. These findings are illustrated in Figure 4.3. Using U.S.-born Hispanic women as an example, the figure shows food stamp benefits at different ages and levels of education. The top line on the chart shows that the highest food stamp benefit—a little over $600 per year when the woman is 20 years old—would be paid if the woman does not finish high school. Interestingly, the next highest benefit would be paid if the woman completes some college, followed by the case in which she graduates high school.

Savings in food stamp benefits paid to women when they raise their level of education are about six to eight times higher than the savings that are realized when men raise their level of education. This gap is primarily driven by the fact that women are far more likely than men to use food stamps. The likelihood of participation for men is not higher than 16 percent for any age, race/ethnicity, and education combination. For women, the rates are as high as 50 percent, for 18-year old black women who do not have a high school diploma, and 32 percent, for their Hispanic counterparts.

While annual expected income from food stamps differs by gender, with women receiving 50 percent to 100 percent more than men, we do not observe a similar differ-

Figure 4.3
Expected Annual Food Stamp Benefits for a U.S.-Born Hispanic Woman

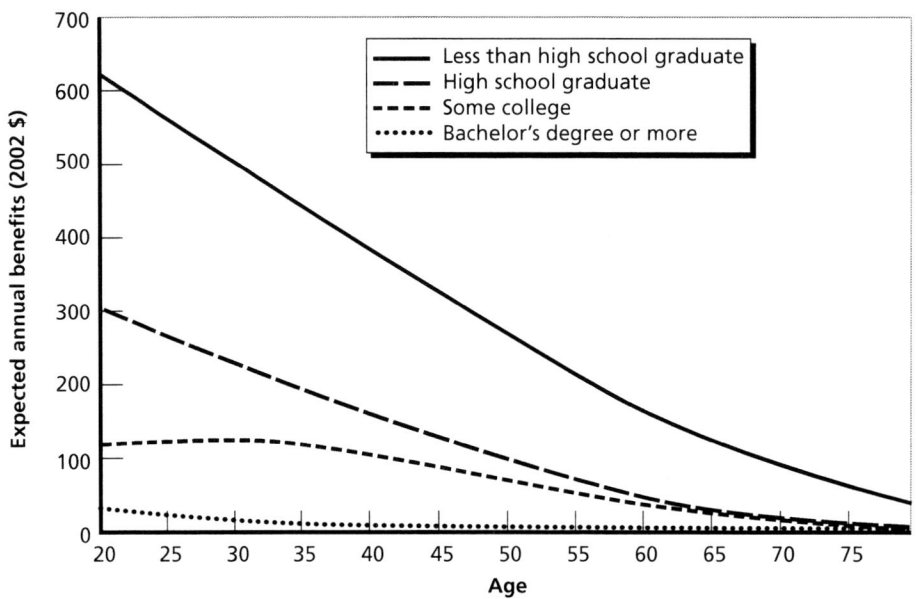

ence statistically across education levels for men. For women, the only practical difference is between college graduates and all other levels of education.

A U.S.-born black woman who graduates from high school rather than dropping out would save the public budget $1,000 per year. On the other hand, U.S.-born white men who graduate from high school rather than dropping out would produce a maximum saving of only $50 per year. Savings for women are highest at age 18 and decrease uniformly with age. Savings for men peak in the mid-forties.

Effects of Educational Attainment on Supplemental Security Income Spending

The SSI program provides an additional safety net to typical Social Security beneficiaries who have limited resources. Eligibility criteria for this assistance program include disability, age over 64, having a blind family member, and the amount of money in bank accounts. The program is administered by the Social Security Administration, with federal and state financing. In our nationally representative data, 4 percent of individuals received SSI benefits for themselves or a dependent. For beneficiaries, SSI income averaged $4,000 per year, with a high of $17,000.

The SIPP data do not indicate whether the SSI benefits paid to a beneficiary were paid for the beneficiary or for a dependent. However, a dependent's eligibility for SSI benefits and amount of benefits paid on behalf of an eligible dependent depend on the dependent's family income. Because more highly educated people earn more, on average, they are less likely to qualify for SSI benefits even if they have a blind dependent.

The results show that, by far, the largest public saving in the SSI program occurs between high school dropouts and high school graduates, across all gender, race/ethnicity, and place-of-birth groups. Gains for women with increased education surpass those of men by 50 to 100 percent, with the exception of Asians, for whom the gain is higher for men. The differential between men and women is driven by the SSI utilization gap between the genders. For male high school dropouts, participation first grows with age, levels out at around age 50, spikes at 65 along with retirement, and falls rather fast as age rises after that point. For female high school dropouts, participation grows with age all the way until retirement age, when it jumps to a different level and then stays mostly flat until death.

As for annual expected SSI income, the major difference in benefits paid to individuals before they are of retirement age is between college graduates and all other education groups, for both men and women. This implies that disability has less drastic effects on the labor market for college graduates than it does for people with less education. This makes sense in that college graduates are likely to have a choice of jobs that are not physically demanding, and a disability would be less likely to restrict job performance. For the post-retirement part of SSI, program income differentials across education levels are not statistically significant.

Not surprisingly, savings typically peak at age 65 for both genders and for all race/ethnicity groups, though for some U.S.-born groups the highest savings occur for individuals in their mid-forties to fifties. Figure 4.4 depicts the expected annual SSI income for a U.S.-born Hispanic woman, at different ages and education levels. The solid line at the top of the chart illustrates the fact that the highest SSI benefits are paid to high school dropouts, no matter what their age. SSI benefits spike for individuals at all education levels at age 65.

Effects of Educational Attainment on Medicaid Spending

Medicaid provides health care benefits to low-income individuals who have no or inadequate medical insurance. While the federal government establishes general guidelines for the administration of Medicaid benefits, eligibility criteria and the scope of services are determined by the states. Accordingly, Medicaid is a joint federal/state program administered by individual states.

Figure 4.4
Expected Annual Supplemental Security Income for a U.S.-Born Hispanic Woman

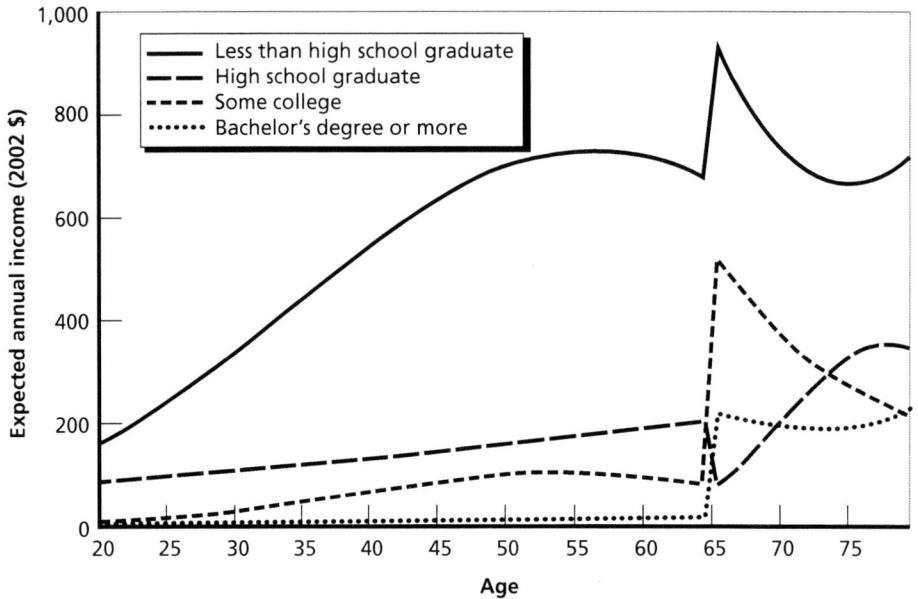

RAND MG686-4.4

In our nationally representative data, 12 percent of individuals utilized Medicaid, and 20 percent of those who utilized the program (2 percent of the total) were hospitalized at the time of the survey.

The results show that, by far, the largest public saving in Medicaid occurs between high school dropouts and high school graduates, across all gender and race/ethnicity groups. The gains for women are generally 50–100 percent higher than those for men, and the highest differential is for Hispanics. Such divergence is observed in inpatient and outpatient services alike; however, the divergence for inpatient services is more critical, since they are almost six times more expensive than outpatient services.

One striking finding about total Medicaid spending is that the burden of men on the system strongly depends on age in addition to educational attainment, while the burden of women is relatively stable, especially for the high school dropout group. One potential explanation relates to pregnancy, as women in their twenties and thirties use Medicare as much as they do in their senior years. Another related finding is that the Medicaid utilization pattern of college-graduate women closely resembles that of men. Women with more education are much more likely to have a job that comes with insurance benefits, and they do not have to rely on Medicaid to finance their health needs.

To illustrate the results, Figure 4.5 shows the Medicaid benefits for a U.S.-born Hispanic woman as a function of age and education level.

**Figure 4.5
Expected Annual Medicaid Benefits for a U.S.-Born Hispanic Woman**

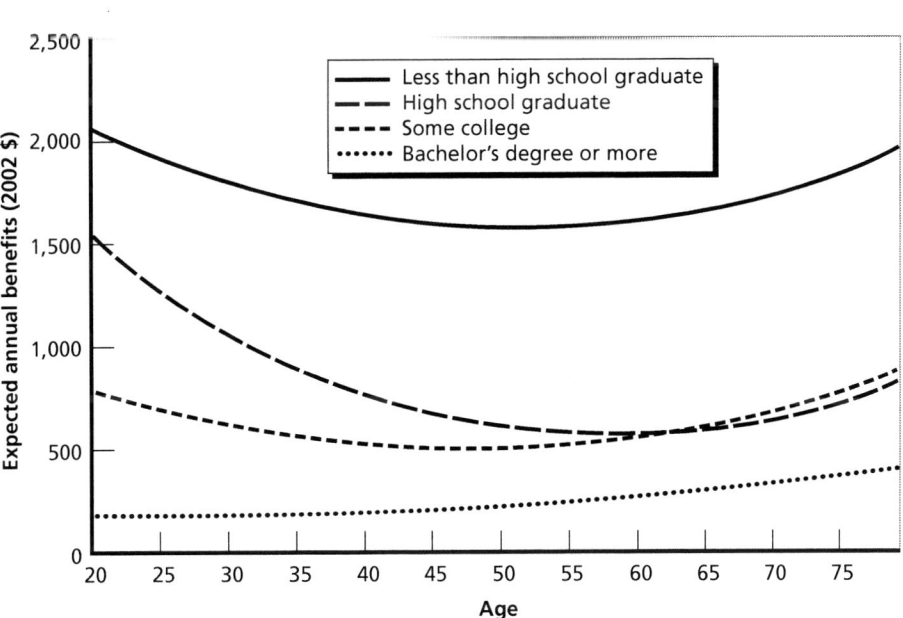

Overall, Medicaid spending decreases with increases in educational attainment at the individual level and offers some of the highest potential savings among all the programs we study.

Further, as noted earlier, the SIPP data do not include institutionalized persons and, consequently, do not include persons in long-term care. Because participation in Medicaid declines with increases in education, we presume that Medicaid spending for long-term care similarly declines with increases in education. If so, our estimates understate the benefits to taxpayers of increased educational attainment.

Effects of Educational Attainment on Medicare Spending

Medicare is a health insurance program for people age 65 or older, disabled people, and patients who have end-stage renal disease. Medicare coverage comprises three parts: Hospital insurance (Part A), Medical Insurance (Part B), and prescription drug insurance (Part D). It is administered by the U.S. Department of Health and Human Services.

In our nationally representative data, 21 percent of individuals utilized Medicare, and 19 percent of those who utilized the program (4 percent of the total) were hospitalized. These figures make Medicare the second most utilized program after Social Security. Our data relate to 2002, so our analysis excludes Medicare Part D, which became available in 2006. Assuming that the educational savings mechanisms in action for Parts A and B would hold true for Part D, public savings computed in this study underestimate current and future Medicare program savings.

Our findings indicate that the effect of educational attainment on Medicare behavior is divided into two groups by age—those age 65 and older and those younger than 65. Below the retirement age of 65, for both genders and all ethnicities, Medicare participation is highly dependent on education level, with clear differences by educational attainment. Although participation rises with age, it is typically below 10 percent for most years.

At age 65, as expected, all subgroups experience a major jump in utilization to 60–95 percent, depending on race/ethnicity. After this point, participation also rises with age; however, the effect of education exhibits a different pattern. For elderly men, there is a clear difference between high school dropouts and graduates as one category and college attendees and graduates as another. For elderly women, there are two clear gaps: between high school dropouts as the first category, high school graduates and some college attendees as the second category, and college degree holders as the third category. The behavior of the second category is closer to the dropout category or the bachelor's category depending on race/ethnicity.

Overall, education affects Medicare spending at the individual level, with the pattern changing depending on age, gender, and race/ethnicity. Figure 4.6 illustrates

Figure 4.6
Expected Annual Medicare Benefits for a U.S.-Born Hispanic Woman

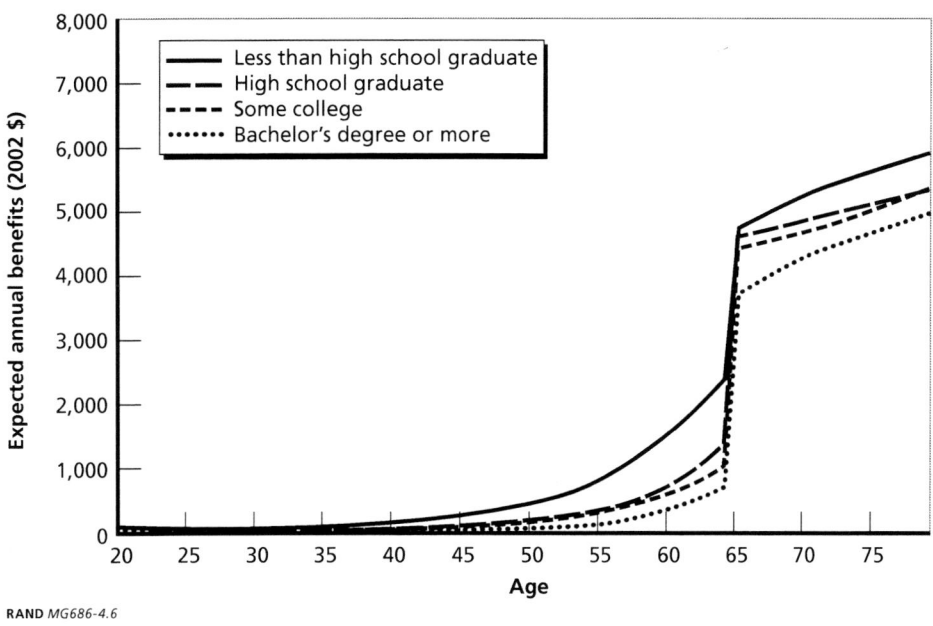

the expected annual Medicare benefits for a U.S.-born Hispanic woman by age and education level.

If a U.S.-born black woman, for whom Medicare payments are the highest, graduated from college rather than dropping out of high school, she would save the Medicare budget $2,300 per year. Savings peak just before age 65 for women and at around age 70 for men.

Overall, Medicare spending is strongly influenced by educational attainment and is relatively insensitive to racial/ethnic and gender differences.

Effects of Educational Attainment on the Costs of Unemployment Insurance

The Unemployment Insurance program provides temporary assistance to workers who "through no fault of their own" are out of a job. Eligibility criteria include having worked in the past year and having earned a threshold level of wage. States administer Unemployment Insurance and set their own thresholds and coverage, though the federal government mandates that benefits can be provided for no more than six months. In our nationally representative data, 4 percent of individuals received Unemployment Insurance benefits. For recipients, Unemployment Insurance income averaged $3,200 per year, with a high of $23,000.

Our findings on unemployment compensation are different from those on social support programs because of the fundamentally different economics of this program. Social support programs are generally means-tested: As the education level of an individual increases, that individual becomes less eligible for the support program. And the amount of a beneficiary's subsidy is not related to how competitive he or she is in the labor market. Unemployment Insurance is an exception in that the level of compensation received depends on the person's last salary, which in turn depends on that person's level of education.

In other words, increased education reduces the likelihood of being unemployed and lowers the utilization of Unemployment Insurance. On the other hand, increased education also increases the amount of the benefit that an individual receives from Unemployment Insurance when he or she does draw on the program.

Our analysis shows that an individual's level of education and gender determine whether or not he or she is likely to use Unemployment Insurance. For men, high school graduates account for the highest spending in the Unemployment Insurance program and high school dropouts account for the lowest for all race/ethnicity groups.

For our example of a U.S.-born Hispanic woman (Figure 4.7), the findings are less clear-cut. Such a woman would account for the highest Unemployment Insurance spending if she is between ages 30 and 50 and has had only some college.

In light of these findings, turning a high school dropout to a college graduate does not seem to yield a saving for the public budget with respect to Unemployment

Figure 4.7
Expected Annual Unemployment Compensation for a U.S.-Born Hispanic Woman

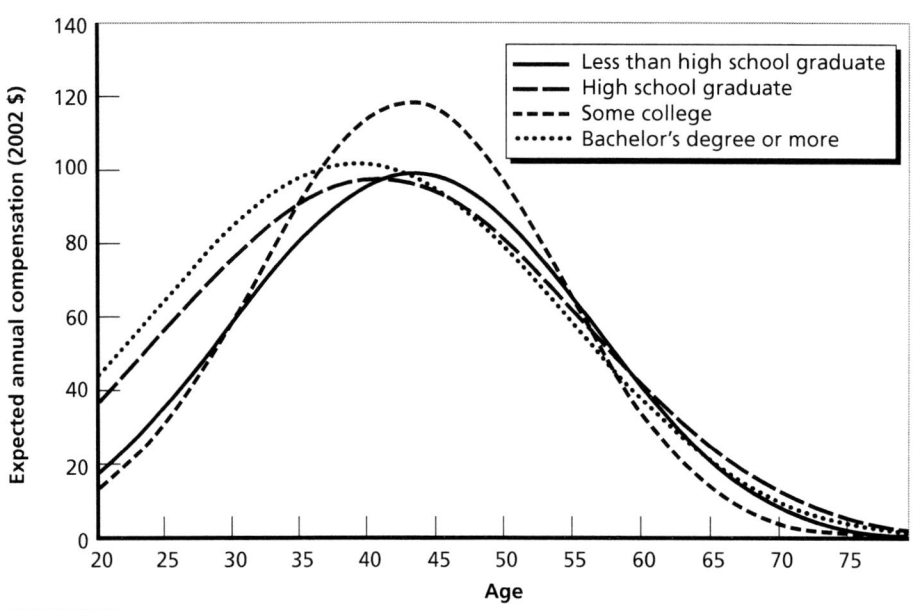

Insurance. However, it does not lead to a drastic increase in spending either, with a maximum difference of $22 per year for men and $48 per year for women.

Effects of Educational Attainment on Social Security Spending

Old-Age, Survivors, and Disability Insurance, or Social Security, as it is more commonly known, is a social insurance program of comprehensive coverage that is intended to replace lost income. Old-age benefits are paid to retired workers who have accumulated enough Social Security credits and are at least 62 years old (credit accumulation can be by the beneficiary or his/her spouse). The level of retirement benefit is a function of the person's earnings history and age at retirement. Early retirement is punished and late retirement is rewarded based on actuarial formulations. "Normal" retirement age is currently 65 but is scheduled to go up to 67 for later cohorts. Survivor's benefits are paid to spouses of at least 60 years of age or children up to 18 years of age who have survived an old-age benefit beneficiary, and to divorcees under some conditions.

In our nationally representative data, 22 percent of individuals received Social Security benefits, which makes Social Security the most used social program. Social Security income averaged $8,400, with a high of $117,000.

As with unemployment compensation, the Social Security program's underlying economics are fundamentally different than the economics of means-tested social support programs. The retirement compensation received under the Social Security retirement subprogram depends on the person's cumulative contribution during the entire time he or she spent in the workforce, which is highly sensitive to that individual's educational attainment.

Expected retirement benefits are higher for people with more education, for all gender and race/ethnicity groups. Moreover, participation in the retirement program is almost universal for men above 65 (the effect of education is statistically insignificant). An interesting finding is that women with some college education appear to have a higher utilization rate than women who graduate from college.

Social Security also furnishes disability and survivor benefits, and this part of the program functions like a typical social support program. Expected benefits are stratified by educational attainment, as survivors and disabled people with more education rely less on Social Security.

A U.S.-born black man who graduates from college rather than dropping out of high school would save the public budget $1,500 per year. His female counterpart would save the public budget $1,300 per year. These savings peak when the individuals are in their early sixties, just before Social Security retirement benefits kick in.

On the other hand, as mentioned above, a similar educational progression leads to higher expected spending under the retirement subprogram. Figure 4.8 shows the annual Social Security benefits for a U.S.-born Hispanic woman, as a function of age and education level.

Figure 4.8
Expected Annual Social Security Benefits for a U.S.-Born Hispanic Woman

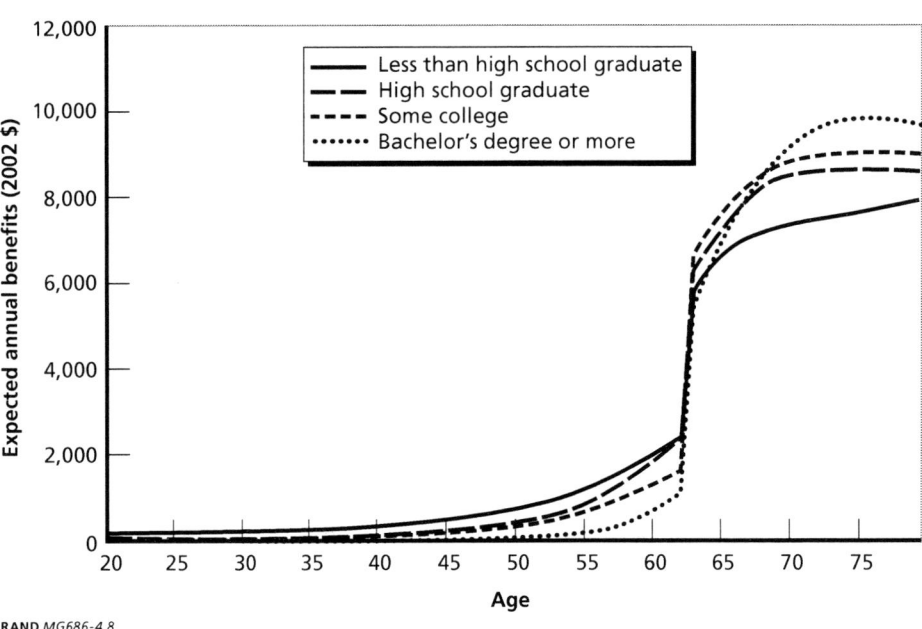

Extra spending reaches a high of $1,150 for U.S.-born white women and $2,500 for their male counterparts. Yet, this additional spending occurs four decades after educational investments are made, and lasts for about two decades only. In contrast, disability and survivor program savings start immediately after educational investments are completed and occur over four decades.

On a present-value basis, the near-term savings in disability and survivor insurance outweigh the long-term extra spending on retirement insurance. This finding holds true for all demographic subgroups and for a wide range of assumptions about the value of money over time. For instance, the net savings is around $3,500 and $2,500 for U.S.-born Hispanic men and women, respectively.

Effects of Educational Attainment on Spending on Social Programs

Figures 4.9 and 4.10 summarize savings in spending on social programs by educational attainment for U.S.-born men and women.

The figures illustrate our finding that the greatest savings in spending on social programs is produced by individuals who graduate from high school rather than dropping out. The savings are the greatest for black and Asian men, at about $40,000, in 2002 dollars, over their lifetimes. High school dropouts have the lowest skill set and

Figure 4.9
2002 Value of Lifetime Decrease in Social Program Spending Resulting from Increased Education for U.S.-Born Men

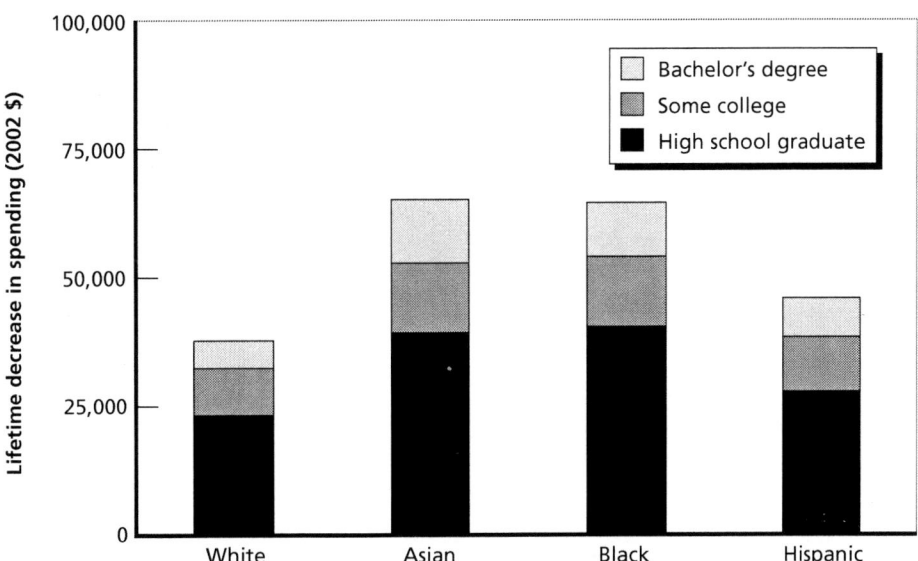

NOTES: The figure shows the value of decreases in spending relative to that for a high school dropout. Dollar amounts are expressed in 2002 dollars discounted to age 18 using a 3 percent real discount rate.
RAND MG686-4.9

demand the lowest wages in the labor market, and therefore they constitute the bulk of the low-income population. Individuals in the "low-income" or "very low-income" groups satisfy the primary eligibility criteria for many social support and insurance programs. High school dropouts are also less likely to hold jobs that offer health insurance, so they are more inclined to rely on government-provided insurance. Further, a disabled individual often cannot perform the manual jobs that are available to people with little education, so disability among high school dropouts is more likely to result in loss of earning power and participation in one or more social support programs.

Beyond the high school diploma, some college seems to have more impact for women and a bachelor's degree seems to have a higher effect for men.

Race/ethnicity also matters. For men and women, Asians and blacks respond most strongly to increased education, with Hispanics following and whites coming in last.

Figure 4.10
2002 Value of Lifetime Decrease in Social Program Spending Resulting from Increased Education for U.S.-Born Women

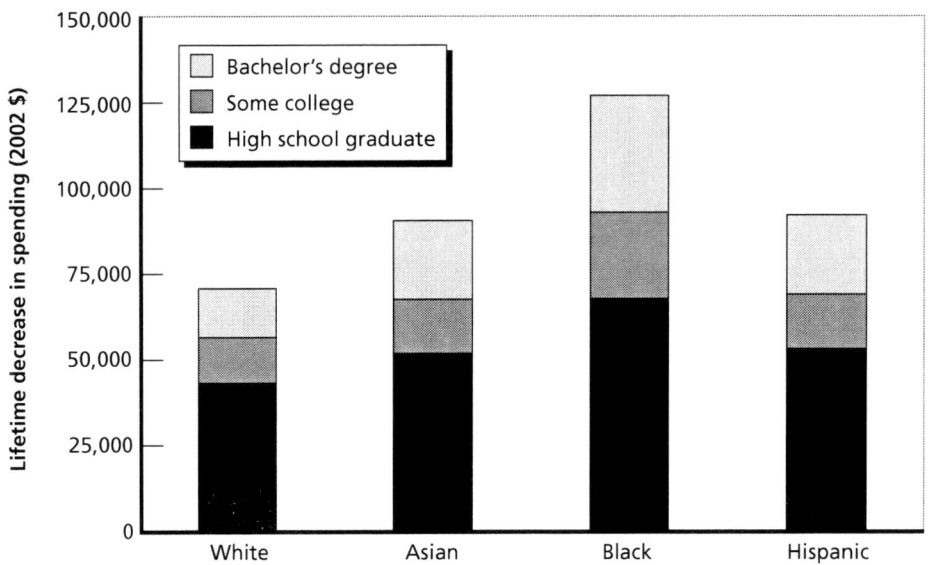

NOTES: The figure shows the value of decreases in spending relative to that for a high school dropout. Dollar amounts are expressed in 2002 dollars discounted to age 18 using a 3 percent real discount rate.
RAND MG686-4.10

Sensitivity Analysis

To explore the extent to which our results are sensitive to our estimates of the effects of education on social program spending, we replicated all the calculations assuming that the effects of increases in education were 25 percent smaller than our estimates. We then calculated the percentage reduction in the estimated effect of an increase in education for each of the demographic populations if the effect of the increase in education on social program spending were only 75 percent of our estimate. Table 4.2 shows the range of percentage reductions in total benefits across the U.S.-born demographic groups for each increase in education level. It also shows the specific demographic group for which the sensitivity to the 25 percent reduction in the estimates of the effects of education was smallest and largest.

Reducing the estimate of the effect of an increase in education from less than high school graduate to high school graduate on social program spending results in roughly the same percentage decrease in estimated total benefits for all demographic groups. The same is true for an increase in education from less than high school graduate to bachelor's degree or more. Increases in education from high school graduate to some college and from some college to bachelor's degree or more have different effects on dif-

Table 4.2
Range of Percentage Reduction in Social Program Spending If Effect of Increased Education Is Reduced 25 Percent, U.S.-Born Men and Women

Increase in Education Level	Percentage Reduction
Less than high school graduate to high school graduate	30 (Hispanic woman) to 33 (white man)
High school graduate to some college	10 (white man) to 21 (black woman)
Some college to bachelor's degree or more	12 (black man) to 20 (white man)
Less than high school graduate to bachelor's degree or more	23 (black woman) to 25 (white man)

ferent demographic groups. Decreases in the estimated effects of increases in education from high school graduate to some college and from some college to bachelor's degree or more generally result in greater reductions in estimated total benefits for men and for whites.

Even if we assume that the estimates of the effects of increased educational attainment are overly optimistic, the results still imply that such increases will yield significant decreases in social program spending. Table 4.3 shows the smallest estimated decrease in social program spending resulting from an increase in education across the U.S.-born demographic groups if the estimate of the effects of the increase in education is reduced 25 percent. In each case, increases in a white man's education would yield the smallest estimated decrease in social program spending.

For example, suppose we assume that our estimate of the effect of increasing education from less than high school graduate to high school graduate on social program spending is 25 percent too high. If we recalculate the effect on social program spend-

Table 4.3
Smallest Estimated Effect of Increased Education on Reduction in Social Program Spending If Effect of Increased Education Is Reduced 25 Percent, U.S.-Born Men and Women

Increase in Education	Smallest Estimated Reduction in Social Program Spending (2002 $, thousands)
Less than high school graduate to high school graduate	15 (white man)
High school graduate to some college	8 (white man)
Some college to bachelor's degree or more	7 (white man)
Less than high school graduate to bachelor's degree or more	28 (white man)

ing assuming that the education effects are 75 percent of our estimates, the lowest estimate of the savings on social program spending that would result from that increase in education is about $15,000 for white, U.S.-born men. The estimated reduction in social program spending for each of the other demographic groups is larger, assuming the effect of increasing education from less than high school graduate to high school graduate is only 75 percent as large as our estimate. The results presented in Table 4.3 show that, even if our estimates of the effects of increases in education on social program spending are significantly too high, such increases will still result in substantial reductions in social program spending to those whose education is increased.

Summary

Increased educational attainment is rewarded in the job market with lower likelihood of being unemployed, higher income when employed, and higher likelihood to have private insurance when employed. Each of these three mechanisms leads to lower demand for support from the government.

The greatest savings in spending on social programs are produced by individuals who graduate from high school rather than dropping out. High school dropouts generally earn low wages and therefore meet the eligibility criteria for many social support programs. High school dropouts are also less likely to hold jobs that offer health insurance, so they are more likely to use government-provided insurance. Beyond the high school diploma, some college seems to have more impact for women, and a bachelor's degree seems to have greater impact for men.

Overall, Medicare spending is influenced by educational attainment and relatively insensitive to racial/ethnic and gender differences.

CHAPTER FIVE

Educational Attainment and Spending on the Corrections System

The inmate population is less educated than the general population. According to a 2003 analysis by the Bureau of Justice Statistics (Harlow, 2003), 40 percent of state prison inmates and 47 percent of jail inmates nationwide have not completed high school. This compares rather strikingly with the 18 percent rate for the general population (Table 5.1).

Investments in education could reduce the demand for correctional capacity. In other words, increased educational attainment yields benefits to taxpayers in the form of savings in the criminal justice system. In this chapter, we examine the effects of educational attainment on public spending for the corrections system.

Appendix D presents the empirical analyses used to estimate the effects of increased educational attainment on incarceration and the resulting costs.

Table 5.1
Educational Attainment for Inmates and the General Population

Education Level	State Prison Inmates (1997)	Jail Inmates (1996)	General Population (1997)
8th grade or less	14.2%	13.1%	7.2%
Some high school	25.5%	33.4%	11.2%
GED	28.5%	14.1%	–
High school graduate	20.5%	25.9%	33.2%
Some college	9.0%	10.3%	26.4%
Bachelor's degree or more	2.4%	3.2%	22.0%
Total	1.1 million	0.5 million	192 million

SOURCE: Harlow (2003).
NOTE: For the general population, individuals with a GED are counted as high school graduates.

Analytic Approach

Public spending for criminal justice includes three broad categories of expenditures: police protection, judicial activities, and corrections. The available research provides strong evidence that more-educated citizens commit less crime and thereby relieve the pressure on the government to strengthen law enforcement, dutifully prosecute suspects, and vigilantly incarcerate wrongdoers.

Because of the difficulty of relating law enforcement and criminal legal proceeding costs to particular incidences of crime or criminals and the resultant lack of structured data related to those, we are unable to address social savings related to the first two expenditure categories. We concentrate on the savings in public spending that result from the effects of increased educational attainment on the costs of incarceration. Basically, policies that improve educational attainment reduce the likelihood of incarceration. This should directly decrease public spending for both the costs of housing prisoners and for building and maintaining correctional facilities.

Federal prisons hold a small share of inmates and account for a small fraction of nationwide incarceration spending (Table 5.2). Therefore, we concentrate on savings on spending on state prisons and county and municipal jails.

Existing studies have certain limitations that preclude their use for our purposes. First, as with the literature on the effect of education on earnings, many studies use years of schooling as the measure of education. We are instead interested in levels of educational attainment. Existing studies also concentrate on two gaps that are most pronounced and perhaps more easily demonstrated statistically: that between high school graduates and dropouts, and that between blacks and whites. Last but not least, almost all research is limited to studying the male half of the population.

We, however, are interested in differences across a fuller range of education levels and racial/ethnic identities and for both genders. Hence, we model per-person correctional spending as the product of per-person incarceration expenditure and likelihood of individual incarceration. This allows us to estimate savings from increased educational attainment for various race/ethnicity and gender combinations, providing more

Table 5.2
Total and Unit Costs of Incarceration, 2002

	Direct Spending ($ million)	Number of Inmates	Annual Cost per Inmate ($)
Federal prisons	4,748	151,618	31,316
State prisons	36,645	1,209,331	30,302
County and municipal jails	18,215	665,475	27,372
Total	59,609	2,026,424	29,416 (average)

SOURCE: Pastore and Maguire (2003).

insight into the nature of this social benefit and potentially providing guidance to more targeted policies.

We use the *Sourcebook of Criminal Justice Statistics, 2003* (Pastore and Maguire, 2003) to compute the per-inmate costs of incarceration. Accordingly, operating the state prison system costs roughly $30,000 per prisoner per year (Table 5.2). Similarly, the local jail system requires expenditures on the order of $27,000 per year per inmate. We assume that savings from education occur because an individual with more education is less likely to be incarcerated. In other words, cost per inmate is assumed to be independent of an inmate's education level.

For state prisons, we use the 1997 administration of the Survey of Inmates in State and Federal Correctional Facilities to estimate the incarcerated population for each education-age-race/ethnicity-gender combination. We also use the 1997 Current Population Survey to estimate general population counts in each corresponding subgroup. Because the Current Population Survey does not include incarcerated persons, we calculate the probability of incarceration as the number of prisoners in each population category divided by the sum of the general population and the number of prisoners for that category.

We follow the same procedure for county and municipal jails, using the 2002 Survey of Inmates of Local Jails and, correspondingly, the 2002 Current Population Survey.

The Effect of Educational Attainment on Crime Rates

Research on the interplay between education and crime dates back at least three decades (Ehrlich, 1975), although a demonstration of a causal effect of education on criminal activity is rather recent (for instance, Lochner and Moretti, 2004). Scholars have long conceptualized why and how education would affect crime and have analyzed nationally representative data to find evidence of the relationship. Freeman (1996) noted that, as of 1993, over two-thirds of incarcerated men lacked a high school diploma. Pettit and Western (2004) concluded that incarceration risks are "highly stratified by education." Not surprisingly, prison inmates average less than 12 years of schooling. Analyses of administrative data on arrests and survey data using reports from the inmates themselves commonly indicate large differences in crime rates among groups of people with different levels of education.

Basically, education reduces the chance that an individual will engage in criminal activity, since education adds to the individual's human capital. The desirable effects of increased human capital occur in a number of different yet complementary and interacting channels.

First, a person with more education is less likely to be unemployed. An individual with a legitimate job has less incentive to engage in crime, everything else constant.

Second, and conversely, the convicted person's criminal record can make it less likely that he or she will be hired and more likely that a job will be low-paying. Former prisoners face more unemployment and earn less compared with similar, nonincarcerated men (Western, Kling, and Weiman [2001] summarize the related literature).

Third, increased educational attainment raises the wage that a person can demand in the labor market. Thus, the value of any lost working time is higher for a person with more education. This, in turn, raises the costs of crime for the individual in several ways. Incarceration means lost time and lost wages from legal activities, as well as a severe reduction in employment following the correctional period. Indeed, empirical evidence showing that higher wages reduce crime is large and growing (e.g., Machin and Meghir, 2000; Viscusi, 1986). This relationship between wages and crime is one reason why older and more educated individuals commit less crime—they stand to lose a lot more in salaries and wages if they are convicted.

On the other hand, an individual's proficiency in committing most types of crime and/or getting away with it does not necessarily rise with more schooling. For instance, reading the works of Shakespeare, understanding how plants derive energy via photosynthesis, or learning what "standard deviation" means do not make a youth better at dealing drugs or mugging people. Hence, the more education a person obtains, the bigger the rift between that person and the attraction of criminal activity.

There may be a relationship between education and white-collar crimes; more-educated people may be better at forgery or embezzlement, for example. However, Lochner (2004) finds that although such a relationship exists, it is not statistically significant. Similarly, Steffensmeier and Demuth (2000) find that more educated federal defendants receive relatively short sentences in general, imposing less cost on the correctional system. It is possible that some specific skills, such as learning the intricacies of financial and management accounting, might make a person a potentially more effective embezzler. However, on average, evidence does not support this idea with regard to education in general. More likely, a small number of large-scale corporate crimes make the headlines, and, as a result, the public forms an impression about the prevalence of white-collar crime that is not supported by the numbers.

A number of recent studies find strong evidence that educational attainment is negatively related to incarceration. Lochner (2004) compares high school graduates to dropouts and finds a causal effect of schooling on various measures of criminal participation, from criminal income to incarceration. He considers in his study other factors that might have an influence on whether or not a high school dropout engages in criminal activity or is incarcerated. These factors include the person's age, personality and other personal characteristics, and conditions in the location where the individual lives. So, controlling for age, individual characteristics, and local conditions, Lochner finds that high school graduates are 81 percent less likely to be incarcerated over a five-year period than dropouts. Similarly, Pettit and Western (2004) find that high school dropouts are about four times more likely to go to prison than high school graduates.

They also note that, while lifetime risk of imprisonment doubled in the two decades leading to 1999, nearly all of the increase was experienced by those who have not gone to college.

Lochner and Moretti (2004) consider the possibility that individuals who are motivated to obtain more schooling have personality characteristics that would prevent them from engaging in criminal activity no matter what, so that even if they dropped out of high school they would not become part of the incarceration statistics. If this were true, then the differences in criminal activity between high school dropouts and high school graduates could not be attributed to more schooling but rather to factors internal to the individuals. However, Lochner and Moretti control for this internal motivation, and they find a causal effect of education on incarceration; in other words, no matter what internal characteristics the individuals have, graduating from high school all by itself makes incarceration less likely.

Using OLS with more covariates than we have, Lochner and Moretti find that, compared with dropping out, high school graduation results in a 0.77 percentage point drop in the probability of imprisonment for white males and a 3.39 percentage point drop in the probability of imprisonment for black males age 20–60. When they instrument for level of education using compulsory schooling laws in states, they find pretty much the OLS effect (0.75 percentage point drop) for white males and about double the OLS effect (7.62 percentage point drop) for black males.

Effects of Educational Attainment on Incarceration Costs

Figures 5.1 and 5.2 summarize the effects of increased educational attainment on the costs of incarceration for U.S.-born men and women. Our estimate for white native-born males (0.68 percent drop) is slightly less than the corresponding Lochner and Moretti estimate. Our estimate for black native-born males (5.88 percent point drop) falls near the center of the corresponding Lochner and Moretti OLS-IV range of estimates.

Savings on the corrections system result primarily from high school graduates, to a lesser extent from those who get some college education, and rather little from college graduates. Even for the highest-risk population subgroups of black and Hispanic men, a bachelor's degree results in just a small nudge upward in social benefits. This is consistent with the human-capital theory of education, since high school dropouts have the lowest skill set, can demand the lowest wages in the labor market, and therefore have the highest incentive to commit crime.

Figure 5.1 shows clearly that the primary benefit from increased education occurs within the black population. On average, the present value (in 2002 dollars) of spending on prisons and jails is reduced by about $85,000 for each U.S.-born black man who graduates from high school rather than dropping out. The savings in prison spending

Figure 5.1
2002 Value of Lifetime Decrease in Incarceration Spending Resulting from Increased Education for U.S.-Born Men

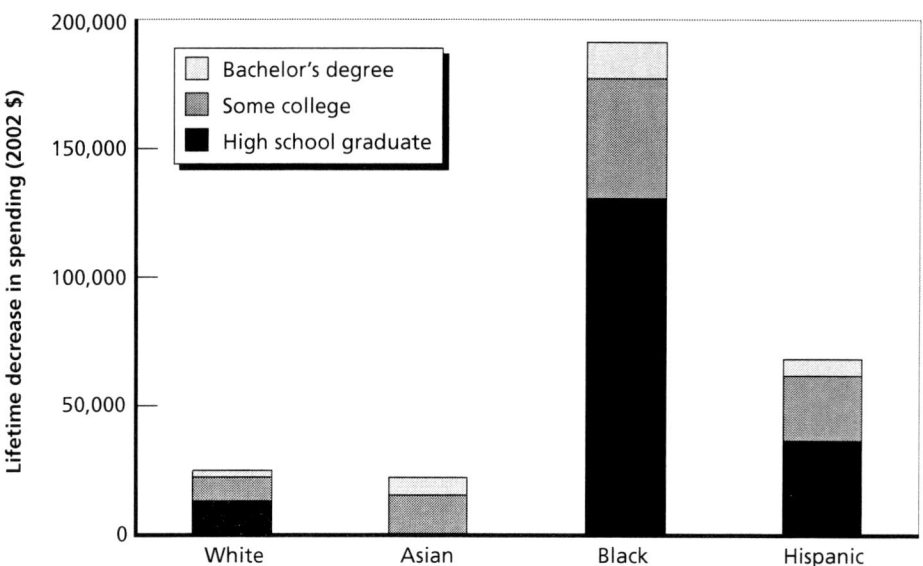

NOTES: The figure shows the value of decreases in spending relative to that for a high school dropout. Dollar amounts are expressed in 2002 dollars discounted to age 18 using a 3 percent real discount rate.
RAND MG686-5.1

that result from increased education by Hispanic men are less than for black men by a large margin, and whites and Asians follow by another large margin.

The leading savings among women are also are expected to occur within the black population, as illustrated by Figure 5.2. However, the magnitude of savings with the female groups is generally about one-tenth that of males. (Note the difference in scale between Figures 5.1 and 5.2.) This naturally parallels the very low incarceration rate of women. While they constitute half of the general population, women make up no more than 6.4 percent of the state prison population and 12 percent of the jail population. Consequently, while the expected savings from reducing incarceration of black and Hispanic women are not negligible by any means, increasing education levels for women would produce a comparatively small part of incarceration-related savings.

The positive effect of education on the public budget through the corrections system incorporates a number of secondary effects that we do not explore here for lack of appropriate data. As mentioned above, ex-inmates earn lower wages following their prison terms, in turn contributing less in tax payments to the public budget for the rest of their lives. Male ex-prisoners are also less likely to share a household with the mothers of their children (Hagan and Dinovitzer, 1999), and their families will likely need more support from social support programs. Therefore, our findings, which are based

Figure 5.2
2002 Value of Lifetime Decrease in Incarceration Spending Resulting from Increased Education for U.S.-Born Women

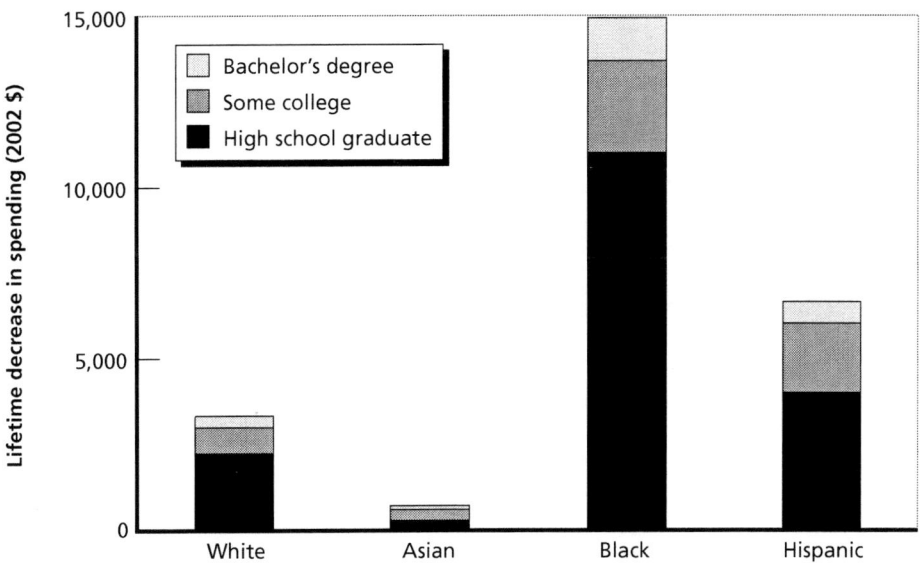

NOTES: The figure shows the value of decreases in spending relative to that for high school dropout. Dollar amounts are expressed in 2002 dollars discounted to age 18 using a 3 percent real discount rate.
RAND MG686-5.2

on only the direct relationship between education and incarceration, constitute a conservative estimate of the social savings through reduced incarceration.

Sensitivity Analysis

We assume that the difference in the probabilities of incarceration between people in a given demographic group at a given age at one level of education and people in that demographic group at that age at a higher level of education reflects the effects of increased educational attainment. We estimate the effects of increased educational attainment on the costs of incarceration as the product of this difference for each demographic group at each age times the average cost of incarceration. Accordingly, changing the estimated effect of increases in educational attainment by 25 percent reduces the resulting estimate by exactly that percentage. A 25 percent reduction in the estimated effect of increases in education on the cost of incarceration yields a 25 percent reduction in the estimate of the reduction in incarceration costs that result from such increases.

Summary

Increases in education would reduce the costs of the criminal justice system and ease the demand for increased capacity in state prisons and county and municipal jails. Table 5.3 shows the total effects of increased education on savings on incarceration spending. It lists the savings that would accrue to the public budget in the extreme case—raising an individual's education from dropping out of high school to college graduate—in each of our population groups. For example, a white U.S.-born man who completes college rather than dropping out of high school would cost taxpayers about $24,000 less (2002 value) in spending on incarceration, on average.

The reductions in incarceration spending from increased education are generally larger for black men and women than for their counterparts. Because women are infrequently incarcerated, the reductions in spending resulting from increases in their education levels are smaller than the savings for men.

Table 5.3
Present Value of Reduced Spending on Incarceration Associated with Increasing Educational Attainment from High School Dropout to College Graduate for U.S.-Born Individuals (2002 $, thousands)

Race/ethnicity	Men	Women
White	23	3
Asian	17	1
Black	137	14
Hispanic	58	6

SOURCE: Appendix D.

CHAPTER SIX

The Costs of Providing Additional Education

In previous chapters, we have described some of the financial benefits that taxpayers will realize if students attain higher levels of education. Presumably, however, those additional years of schooling will also cost money. In this chapter, we identify what the costs of providing additional schooling would be. As noted in Chapter One, we do not address the question of what could be done to induce students to continue their education to a higher level or what such efforts would cost. Rather, we focus on the benefits taxpayers would realize if students increased their education net of the costs of providing the increases in education.

The relevant cost concept is that of "marginal" cost: the cost of providing education to one additional student. Marginal cost will typically be lower than average cost because several expense items (such as a principal's salary) are fixed regardless of the number of students enrolled. However, data on the marginal costs of education are generally not available. Accordingly, we estimated the costs of raising a person's education level based on what the average costs are per student at each level of education. Because average costs are typically larger than are marginal costs, our estimates overestimate the costs of providing education to an additional student and, consequently, underestimate the net benefits to taxpayers of increased education.

The costs of education vary from state to state and within states, by type of institution, and by level of education. We used national average operating cost estimates for U.S. public high schools and colleges to estimate the costs of providing increased education and, consequently, taxpayers' net benefits from increased educational attainment. For the public secondary education system, per-pupil spending figures are based on average daily attendance (ADA), the average number of students who attended school on each day of the school year. At the postsecondary level, because college students can enroll for a full course load or for individual classes, per-pupil spending figures are based on full-time equivalent (FTE) students: the total number of enrollments in all courses divided by the number of courses taken by a full-time student.

We used SIPP data collected in 2002 to estimate the benefits that taxpayers would realize from increases in education. The closest corresponding school year is the 2001–2002 school year. In that school year, the national average expenditure per ADA in public K–12 education was $7,727 (U.S. Department of Education, National

Center for Education Statistics, 2007, Table 33, p. 46). Assuming that K–12 school districts can generally accommodate some increases in enrollment without additional construction, we estimate that the cost of additional education in secondary schools will average about $7,700 per pupil ADA. If a student were to complete high school rather than dropping out, taxpayers would have to pay roughly $15,000, in 2002 dollars discounted to age 18, to pay for the additional schooling.

In the 2000–2001 school year, the most recent school year for which data were available, public two-year colleges' current expenditures averaged about $9,400 per FTE pupil (U.S. Department of Education, National Center for Education Statistics, 2007, Table 346, p. 500). Two-year colleges' tuition and fees that year averaged about $1,800 per FTE (U.S. Department of Education, National Center for Education Statistics, 2007, Table 320, p. 467). We assume that virtually all two-year colleges' expenditures are for educational activities and that federal, state, and local government appropriations provide the difference between two-year colleges' average current expenses and students' tuition and fees. Accordingly, it would cost taxpayers about $7,600 per FTE to provide additional education in a two-year college.

We assume that students who are induced to obtain some college rather than terminating their education at high school graduation will generally attend lower-cost institutions that are relatively close to their homes. Accordingly, we assume that increasing education from high school graduation to some college will cost taxpayers about $15,000, in 2002 dollars, to pay for the increase in education.

In the 2000–2001 school year, public four-year colleges' current expenditures averaged about $28,000 per FTE pupil (U.S. Department of Education, National Center for Education Statistics, 2007, Table 346, p. 500). Students' tuition and fees that year averaged about $7,800 per FTE (U.S. Department of Education, National Center for Education Statistics, 2007, Table 320, p. 467). Public four-year institutions' current revenues other than tuition and fees are equally divided between sources of revenues that contribute, at least in part, to the costs of educating students (federal, state, and local government appropriations; private gifts, grants, and contracts; and endowment income) and revenues from sources (federal, state, and local government grants; contracts; federally funded research and development centers; independent operations; and sales and services) that generally support expenditures on activities other than education. If all the funds provided by the first group of sources are used to support educational expenses, taxpayers spent about $10,100 per FTE student in public four-year institutions for educational purposes. We assume that it would cost taxpayers about $10,000 per FTE to provide additional education in a four-year public college or university. We estimate that increasing education from some college to a college degree will cost taxpayers about $20,000 in 2002 dollars.

Finally, the extreme example we consider is increasing a student's education from high school dropout to college graduate. This would entail two more years of high school and four years of college. The costs of providing this increase would be spread over six years. The discounted present value of the cost of this increase in education would be about $47,000 in 2002 dollars.

Research has shown that the average cost of education per student falls as the number of students in a school or district rises. To the extent that educational attainment is increased by adding students to the existing educational infrastructure, the cost of education we use is an overestimate of the costs taxpayers would incur to increase education. For policy goals that would result in a large increase in enrollment, capacity may need to be expanded through new investments. In this case, the use of current average cost will certainly be more appropriate than current marginal cost. Across both cases, our practice of using average rather than marginal costs in our estimates implies that our net benefit calculations are lower bounds.

over six years. The discounted present value of the cost of this increase in education would be about $47,000 in 2002 dollars.

Research has shown that the average cost of education per student falls as the number of students in a school or district rises. To the extent that educational attainment is increased by adding students to the existing educational infrastructure, the cost of education we use is an overestimate of the costs taxpayers would incur to increase education. For policy goals that would result in a large increase in enrollment, capacity may need to be expanded through new investments. In this case, the use of current average cost will certainly be more appropriate than current marginal cost. Across both cases, our practice of using average rather than marginal costs in our estimates implies that our net benefit calculations are lower bounds.

CHAPTER SEVEN
Educational Attainment and Public Revenues and Costs

The preceding chapters provide estimates of the benefits that taxpayers would receive from increases in educational attainment and the costs that would be incurred in providing the additional education. In this chapter, we review the estimates and then combine them to assess the total and net benefits to taxpayers of raising educational attainment.

Effects of Increases in Education on the Public Budget

Tax Payments

Greater educational attainment increases both the likelihood of employment and an individual's earnings when employed. The higher income realized by more highly educated people results in higher tax payments and higher payments to social support and insurance programs, such as Social Security and Medicare.

Increases in the education level of individuals in every population subgroup result in substantial increases in payments into tax and social service programs by more-educated persons. For example, compared with the average high school dropout, the average college graduate contributes to the public budget additional taxes whose present value (2002 dollars) varies between $120,000 and $192,000, depending on demographics.

Graduating from college rather than ending education with only some college provides the largest impact on tax payments, followed by earning a high school diploma rather than dropping out of high school. The difference between the tax payments made by a person with a high school diploma and an otherwise similar person with some college is smaller, but still substantial.

Whites and Asians contribute the most to the tax system as a result of increased education. Also, the variability of the taxation increment by race/ethnicity is more pronounced for earning a bachelor's degree compared with a high school diploma or some college education. Finally, our results indicate lower increases in tax payments as a result of increases in educational attainment for women compared with men. However, this finding should be interpreted with caution, since we divide tax payments (apart from payroll taxes) evenly within a household, regardless of gender. Therefore, this finding does not necessarily reflect a gender-wage gap.

Spending on Social Support and Insurance Programs
Because greater educational attainment increases both the likelihood of employment and an individual's earnings when employed, increases in education level both reduce the likelihood that a person will rely on public support and (with the exception of Unemployment Insurance and Social Security) decrease the amount of benefit a person will receive from public programs upon participation. We examined the effects of increased educational attainment on program spending for eight of the largest social support and insurance programs for which sufficient data on program participation and program spending are available.

We found that the greatest savings on spending for social programs results from graduating from high school rather than dropping out. This is not surprising, as high school dropouts generally earn low wages and therefore meet the eligibility criteria for many social support and insurance programs. High school dropouts are also less likely to hold jobs that offer health insurance, so they are more inclined to rely on government-provided insurance. Beyond the high school diploma, some college seems to have more impact for women, and a bachelor's degree seems to have a higher effect for men.

Race/ethnicity matters. For men, Asians and blacks generate larger social program savings with increased education, followed by Hispanics, with whites coming in last. For women, blacks again stand out in terms of the savings they would create by increasing their education level, followed by Asians and Hispanics at about the same level, and by whites again as a distant last.

Incarceration Costs
More-educated citizens commit less crime. Consequently, increases in educational attainment reduce the likelihood of criminal activity and, consequently, incarceration. This decreases the need for public spending for building and operating correctional facilities. Because federal prisons hold a small share of inmates and account for a small fraction of nationwide incarceration, we concentrated on savings on spending on state prisons and on county and municipal jails.

For both men and women, the primary savings on the costs of incarceration result from increased education within the black population. Hispanics trail blacks by a large margin, with whites and Asians following by another large margin. However, the magnitude of savings with each female group is generally about one-tenth of those of the corresponding male group.

The benefit to increasing education from the corrections system is greatest for graduating from high school rather than dropping out, less from getting some college education rather than none, and rather little from graduating from college compared with getting only some college. Even for the highest-risk population subgroups of black and Hispanic men, a bachelor's degree results in just a small increase in incarceration savings over some college. This is consistent with the human capital theory of education, as high school dropouts have the lowest skill set and demand the lowest wages in the labor market, and therefore have the highest financial incentive to commit crime.

Costs of Increased Education

Achieving an increase in educational attainment will require higher spending to provide the additional education. We assume that the costs of raising a person's education level equal the current national average operating costs per student at each level of education. We use the national average cost per student in high schools as our estimate of the public cost of additional high school education. We use the national average public cost per FTE student in public two-year colleges as our estimate of the cost to taxpayers of providing college education for two years following high school graduation. We use the national average public cost per FTE student in public four-year colleges as our estimate of the cost taxpayers would incur to provide education in college after the first two years. We assume that the average costs are independent of student characteristics.

Net Benefits from Increased Educational Attainment

The net benefit to taxpayers of increased educational attainment equals the sum of the benefits we have considered in our study minus the costs of providing the additional education. We have focused on only those benefits for which data are readily available: increases in the public budget through increased tax revenues, reductions in spending on social support and insurance programs, and reductions in public spending on the corrections system. The estimates presented below understate the net benefits of increased educational attainment to the extent that the benefit categories we did not consider due to lack of data would produce additional savings.

Both the costs of providing additional education and the benefits are incurred in the future. The costs are incurred in the first few years after an individual decides to continue his or her education, while he or she is in school. Taxpayers do not realize the benefits of increased educational attainment until future years, when the more-educated individuals pay more in taxes, place fewer demands on social support programs, and do not engender incarceration costs. Hence, we discount both the costs of increased educational attainment and the benefits occurring in the future to the present (i.e., the time investment begins). Because much of our data are for 2002, we discount all monetary amounts to 2002.

For this analysis, all costs and benefits are treated as incremental and relative to the respective baseline of the increase in attainment. For instance, if we want to assess the benefit to taxpayers if a student achieves a high school diploma rather than dropping out, the benefit is the difference in expected tax payments, social program costs, and the costs of incarceration between the average high school graduate and the average high school dropout, and not simply the expected values for high school graduates per se. We apply a similar logic to all costs and benefits.

Table 7.1 illustrates the study's basic calculation. It shows the present value of the total and net benefits to taxpayers, in 2002 dollars, of increasing a U.S.-born white male's education from high school dropout to high school graduate. Tables 7.2–7.5 provide the corresponding estimates for each of the groups for each of four increments in education: high school dropout to high school graduate, high school graduate to some college, some college to college graduate, and high school dropout to college graduate.

Our estimates show that if the average U.S.-born white male high school dropout were to continue his education through high school graduation, he would pay additional taxes and Social Security and Medicare payments over his lifetime. These additional payments into the public treasury would be worth about $54,000. He would also draw, on average, about $22,000 less from the public treasury in social program benefits and reduce demands on the public treasury for prison and jail costs by about $13,000, on average. In all, the public treasury would need about $89,000 less from taxpayers, on average, for each U.S.-born white male who completes high school rather than dropping out.

If a would-be high school dropout completes high school instead, the taxpayers will have to pay about $15,000 to pay for the additional schooling, so the taxpayers net benefit if a high school dropout goes on to graduate instead is about $74,000.

Table 7.2 shows the benefits to taxpayers of increasing education from high school dropout to high school graduate. Increases in a man's education from high school

Table 7.1
Effects of Increasing Education from High School Dropout to High School Graduate on Public Revenues and Costs for a U.S.-Born White Male

Type of Increase or Cost	Amount (2002 $, thousands)
Increases to public budget	
Increased tax payments	54
Reduced spending on social programs	22
Reduced spending on incarceration	13
Total increases in public budget	89
Cost of providing additional education	15
Net benefit to taxpayers	74

SOURCE: Appendixes B, C, and D.

Table 7.2
Benefits to Taxpayers from Increasing Educational Attainment from Less Than High School to High School Graduate, U.S.-Born Men and Women (2002 $, thousands)

	Increased Tax Payments	Reduced Social Program Spending	Reduced Incarceration Spending	Total Benefit	Net Benefit Estimated	Net Benefit 25 Percent Reduction
Whites						
Men	54	22	13	89	74	51
Women	50	41	2	93	78	54
Asians						
Men	50	37	1	89	74	51
Women	52	49	0	101	86	60
Blacks						
Men	40	38	123	201	186	134
Women	38	64	10	113	98	69
Hispanics						
Men	46	26	35	107	92	64
Women	44	50	4	98	83	57

SOURCE: Appendixes B, C, and D.

dropout to high school graduate generally yield greater benefits to taxpayers than do comparable increases in a woman's education. The benefits to increased education do not differ much across racial/ethnic groups.

Table 7.2 also shows what would be the net benefit to taxpayers if the effects of an increase in education on public revenues and costs were 25 percent smaller than our estimates. With a 25-percent-smaller estimate of the effect of education level, the net benefit to increasing a person's education from high school dropout to high school graduate would be 14 to 37 percent smaller. Even if our estimates of the effects of the increase in education on public revenues and costs were 25 percent too high, taxpayers would realize net benefits to an increase in education level from high school dropout to high school graduate of at least $51,000 (U.S.-born Asian man) and as much as $134,000 (U.S.-born black man).

Table 7.3 shows the benefits to taxpayers of increasing education from high school graduate to some college. Increases in a man's education from high school graduate to some college generally yield somewhat greater benefits to taxpayers than do comparable increases in a woman's education. The benefits to increased education do not differ much across racial/ethnic groups.

Here, too, we conducted a sensitivity analysis to determine the extent to which the estimated effect of the increase in education on net benefits to taxpayers was sensi-

Table 7.3
Benefits to Taxpayers from Increasing Educational Attainment from High School Graduate to Some College, U.S.-Born Men and Women (2002 $, thousands)

	Increased Tax Payments	Reduced Social Program Spending	Reduced Incarceration Spending	Total Benefit	Net Benefit Estimated	25 Percent Reduction
Whites						
Men	36	9	9	54	39	26
Women	40	12	1	52	37	24
Asians						
Men	34	13	15	63	47	33
Women	41	14	0	55	40	26
Blacks						
Men	27	14	46	87	68	51
Women	30	22	3	55	40	27
Hispanics						
Men	31	10	25	66	50	36
Women	35	15	2	52	37	24

SOURCE: Appendixes B, C, and D.

tive to our estimates of the effects of the increase in education on public revenues and costs. Table 7.3 shows that the net benefit of increasing a person's education from high school graduate to some college would be 15 to 40 percent smaller than our estimate if the effect of the increase in education on public revenues and costs were 25 percent less than our estimates. Even if our estimates of the effects of the increase in education on public revenues and costs were 25 percent too high, taxpayers would realize net benefits from an increase in education level from high school graduate to some college of at least $24,000 (U.S.-born white or Hispanic woman) and as much as $51,000 (U.S.-born black man).

Table 7.4 shows the benefits to taxpayers of increasing education from some college to college graduate. Increases in a man's education from some college to college graduate generally yield slightly greater benefits to taxpayers than do comparable increases in a woman's education. The benefits to increased education do not differ much across racial/ethnic groups.

Table 7.4 also shows that, if the effect of the increase in education on public revenues and costs were 25 percent less than our estimates, the net benefit to increasing a person's education level from some college to college graduate would be 28 to 38 percent smaller. Even if our estimates of the effects of the increase in education level on public revenues and costs were 25 percent too high, taxpayers would realize net benefits

Table 7.4
Benefits to Taxpayers from Increasing Educational Attainment from Some College to College Graduate, U.S.-Born Men and Women (2002 $, thousands)

	Increased Tax Payments	Reduced Social Program Spending	Reduced Incarceration Spending	Total Benefit	Net Benefit Estimated	Net Benefit 25 Percent Reduction
Whites						
Men	117	9	3	129	109	71
Women	89	14	0	103	83	53
Asians						
Men	111	15	6	133	113	74
Women	91	22	0	113	93	61
Blacks						
Men	89	15	15	118	90	66
Women	68	32	1	102	82	56
Hispanics						
Men	102	10	6	119	99	64
Women	79	22	1	102	82	53

SOURCE: Appendixes B, C, and D.

to an increase in education from some college to college graduate of at least $53,000 (white or Hispanic woman) and as much as $74,000 (Asian man).

Finally, Table 7.5 summarizes the results of the taxpayers' benefit calculations for each population group under the most extreme scenario—raising an individual's educational attainment from less than high school graduate to college graduate.

The present value (2002 dollars) of the benefits to taxpayers from increasing educational attainment from high school dropout to college graduate range from about $187,000 to $341,000 per individual, depending on the population group. After subtracting the present value of the costs of providing the additional education—$47,000 per college graduate—these figures translate to expected average net benefits of $123,000–$240,000 for each person who increases his or her education from high school dropout to college graduate.

The sum of the estimates for a given type of benefit and population group in Tables 7.2, 7.3, and 7.4 do not exactly equal the corresponding estimate in Table 7.5 because of differences in the assumed time at which the benefits from each increase in education level begin. The estimates in Tables 7.2, 7.3, and 7.4 each reflect the effects of two years of additional schooling, so the increase in educational attainment begins to yield benefits two years after the additional schooling begins. The estimates in Table 7.5 each assume six years of additional schooling, so the increase in educational attainment

Table 7.5
Benefits to Taxpayers from Increasing Educational Attainment from High School Dropout to College Graduate, U.S.-Born Men and Women (2002 $, thousands)

	Increased Tax Payments	Reduced Social Program Spending	Reduced Incarceration Spending	Total Benefit	Net Benefit Estimated	Net Benefit 25 Percent Reduction
Whites						
Men	192	38	23	254	206	138
Women	167	64	3	234	187	123
Asians						
Men	181	63	21	266	219	147
Women	171	82	1	254	207	139
Blacks						
Men	144	64	179	388	341	240
Women	128	114	14	256	209	143
Hispanics						
Men	165	45	64	274	228	154
Women	148	83	6	237	190	127

SOURCE: Appendixes B, C, and D.

begins to yield benefits six years after the additional schooling begins. Because the future benefits to additional schooling are discounted to age 18 in 2002 dollars, the estimates reflect differences in the times when benefits begin.

Table 7.5 also shows that, if the effect of the increase in education on public revenues and costs were 25 percent less that our estimates, the net benefit to increasing a U.S.-born person's education from high school dropout to college graduate would be 19 to 36 percent smaller. Even if our estimates of the effects of the increase in education level on public revenues and costs were 25 percent too high, taxpayers would realize net benefits to an increase in education from high school dropout to college graduate of at least $123,000 (white women) and as much as $240,000 (black man).

The Effects of Increased Educational Attainment: An Example

We use the results for a U.S.-born Hispanic woman to illustrate the results of our analysis. Recall that we examine the benefits to taxpayers from increased educational attainment and the costs that taxpayers would incur to provide increased education. We do not consider the costs of any policies or programs undertaken to induce individuals to increase their education. Also, recall that the computations are mortality-adjusted. In other words, the figures include the schedule of expected age at death, as of 2002, for each population subgroup in the United States. Assuming that life expectancy will continue to increase, our calculations constitute a conservative estimate for expected future benefits.

Figure 7.1 compares the discounted present values (2002 dollars) of the costs and benefits that taxpayers would receive if a U.S.-born Hispanic women were to complete college rather than drop out of high school. The public savings from social support programs alone more than compensate for the cost of providing the additional education. While the criminal justice system benefit is minor for this specific population group, substantial benefits from increased tax payments help the educational investment to generate a net benefit to taxpayers in excess of about $190,000.

The results presented in Figure 7.1 reflect one scenario: that of raising a Hispanic woman's education level from less than high school graduate to college graduate. We now turn to some alternative scenarios, raising a man or woman's education level from

- high school dropout to high school graduate
- high school graduate to some college
- some college to college graduate.

Figure 7.1
Benefits and Costs of Raising the Education of a U.S.-Born Hispanic Woman from Less Than High School Graduate to College Graduate

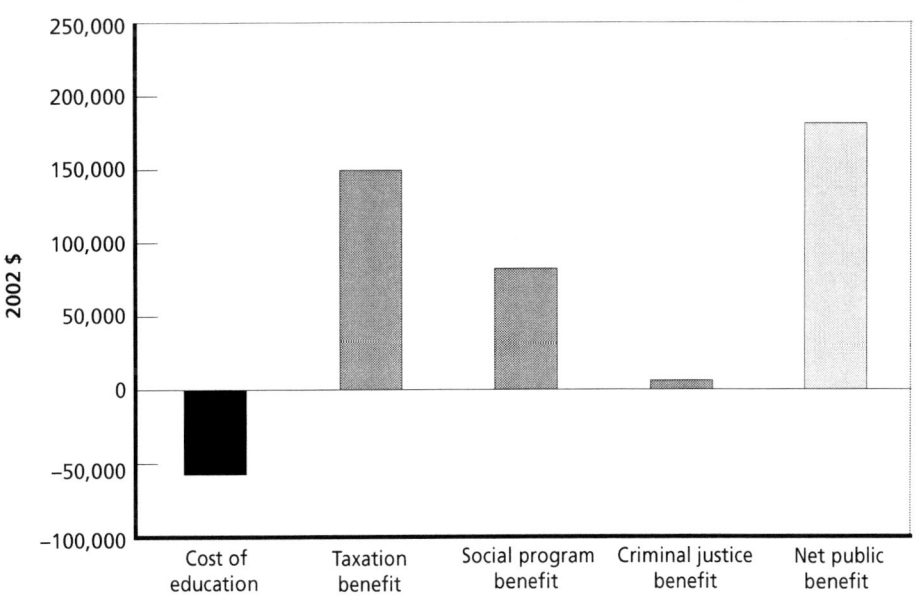

SOURCE: Appendixes B, C, and D.

Table 7.6 summarizes the results by scenario. Increased education generally yields greater net benefits for Hispanic men than for Hispanic women.

Sensitivity Analysis

To explore the extent to which our results are sensitive to the estimates of the effects of education on net benefits to taxpayers, we replicated all the calculations, this time assuming that the effects of increases in education on each type of benefit to taxpayers were 25 percent smaller than our estimates. We then calculated the percentage reduction in the estimated effect of an increase in education for each of the demographic populations if the effect of the increase in education on tax payments, social program costs, and incarceration costs were only 75 percent as large as our estimate. In the recalculations, we assume the costs of providing the additional education are the same as in our original estimates. Table 7.7 shows the range of percentage reductions in net benefits to taxpayers across the demographic groups for each increase in the level of education.

Table 7.6
Net Benefits from Increased Educational Attainment Among U.S.-Born Hispanics (2002 $, thousands)

Increase in Educational Attainment	Men	Women
From high school dropout to college graduate	228	190
From high school dropout to high school graduate	92	83
From high school graduate to some college	50	37
From some college to college graduate	90	82

SOURCE: Appendixes B, C, and D.

Table 7.7
Range of Percentage Reduction in Net Benefits to Taxpayers If the Effect of Increased Education Is Reduced 25 Percent

Increase in Education Level	Percentage Reduction
Less than high school graduate to high school graduate	28 (black man) to 34 (Asian man)
High school graduate to some college	29 (black man) to 36 (white woman)
Some college to bachelor's degree or more	32 (black woman) to 37 (white woman)
Less than high school graduate to bachelor's degree or more	29 (black man) to 34 (white woman)

Reducing the estimate of the effect of an increase in education on net benefits to taxpayers by 25 percent has largely the same result for every demographic group, although the effects are slightly smaller for the estimates of net benefits for black males and somewhat greater for those of white women. The range of percentage reductions in net benefits across the groups is generally narrow. Reducing the estimated effect of increased education level generally has roughly the same effect on the net benefits estimates for each increase in education considered here.

Even if we assume that the estimates of the effects of increased educational attainment are overly optimistic, the results still imply that such increases yield significant net benefits to taxpayers. Table 7.8 shows the smallest estimated increase in net benefits resulting from an increase in education across the demographic groups if the estimate of the effects of the increase in education on tax payments, social program costs, and incarceration costs is reduced 25 percent.

For example, suppose we assume that our estimate of the effect of increasing education from less than high school graduate to high school graduate on net benefits to taxpayers is 25 percent too high. If we recalculate the effect on tax payments, social program costs, and incarceration costs assuming that the education effects are 75 percent of our estimates and assume no change in the costs of providing the additional education, the lowest estimate of the increase in total benefits that would result from that increase in education is about $51,000 (Asian man and white man). The estimated increase in net benefits for each of the other demographic groups, assuming that the effect of increasing education from less than high school graduate to high school graduate is only 75 percent as large as our estimate, is larger.

The results presented in Table 7.8 show that even if our estimates of the effects of increases in education on net benefits to taxpayers are substantially too high, increases in educational attainment will still result in substantial benefits to taxpayers in the form of increased public revenues and decreased public costs by those whose education is increased.

Table 7.8
Smallest Estimated Effect of Increased Education on Net Benefits If Effect of Increased Education Is Reduced

Increase in Education	Smallest Estimated Effect on Net Benefits to Taxpayers (2002 $, thousands)
Less than high school graduate to high school graduate	51 (Asian man and white man)
High school graduate to some college	24 (Hispanic woman and white woman)
Some college to bachelor's degree or more	53 (Hispanic woman and white woman)
Less than high school graduate to bachelor's degree or more	123 (white woman)

Putting the Estimates in Perspective

As noted above, we use data collected in 2002 to estimate the models used in this analysis. In doing so, we assume that the estimated relationships between education level and governmental revenues and costs will remain approximately the same into the future. Specifically, we assume that the effects of education on income and, consequently, on tax payments and participation in social programs, in the future will be generally the same as the effects observed in 2002. We also assume that federal, state, and local tax structures, social support programs, and incarceration patterns will not change substantially in the future.

The level of education needed to succeed in labor markets has been increasing for decades. And the income gaps between individuals with differing levels of education have consequently grown consistently over time. It seems likely that the gaps that existed in 2002, when the data used to estimate our models were collected will, if anything, widen into the future. If they do so, the effects of education on government revenues and costs will exceed the estimates presented here.

Federal and state tax structures are changed from time to time, but the changes are generally marginal. The overall structure has not been significantly changed for decades. Similarly, the rates and ceilings that determine Social Security and Medicare contributions have been increased over time, but the general structure of the systems remain the same. If anything, the growing federal budget deficit and growing concerns for the future of the Social Security and Medicare systems as baby boomers begin to reach retirement suggest that the payroll taxes levied to support these programs will increase over time. If that occurs, the estimates presented here will understate the effects of increases in educational attainment on contributions to government revenues.

It is obviously possible that the structure of one or more of the social programs we consider here will be significantly modified sometime in the future. Recent changes (such as the welfare reform of the 1990s) generally reflect concerns that these programs were too often used by people who did not need the support offered by the programs. This suggests that any future changes are more likely to further reduce access to these programs. If so, increases in the income differential associated with increases in education will result in greater reductions in social program participation and, consequently, greater costs than the estimates presented here.

Changes in some of these relationships are likely to occur at some future date. Consequently, the estimates presented here cannot be viewed as precise. However, the magnitudes of the estimates are generally so large that even changes that substantially reduce the effects of increases in educational attainment on government revenues and costs will not reduce the effects of such increases to zero. Moreover, changes that increase the effects of education on government revenues and costs are more likely than are changes that reduce the effects. If such changes occur, the estimates presented here will understate the effects of increased educational attainment on government revenues and costs.

As discussed in Chapter Two, our analysis assumes that the relationships observed in the data are causal. That is, we assume that the differences in contributions to government revenues and costs between more highly educated and less highly educated people are the result of the differences in their levels of education. There is abundant evidence that greater educational attainment leads to increases in earnings and that earnings are related to contributions to government revenues and costs. It is possible that some other factor is related to both the level of an individual's education and his or her contributions to government revenues and costs. But it is clear that education is a dominant factor, even if there are others. Moreover, the magnitude of the effect of education on earnings has grown consistently over time. Because we assume the relationships between education and contributions to government revenues and costs that existed in 2002 will continue over time, our estimates do not reflect the effects of increases in the effect of education on earnings and, consequently, on government revenues and costs.

The bottom line is that the analyses presented below, notwithstanding the inherent uncertainties in estimating future trends and patterns, show that increasing education will yield significant benefits to taxpayers. We recognize that the greatest gains accrue to those whose education levels are improved and that increases in educational attainment also provide numerous types of noneconomic benefits in addition to economic benefits. However, this analysis indicates that the effects of raising an individual's level of education creates high benefits for the public budget which should be considered in assessing the importance of finding, funding, and implementing programs for increasing education levels.

Summary

This analysis indicates that increases in a native-born student's education level create high net benefits for the public budget, regardless of the student's gender and race/ethnicity. Data limitations preclude detailed conclusions regarding the effects of increases in an immigrant's education level. The limited research we conducted regarding the effects of increasing immigrants' education on the public budget suggests that increases in an immigrant's education will also yield significant benefits to taxpayers.

Policies and programs that succeed in encouraging students to increase their educational attainment will yield long-term and substantial financial benefits to taxpayers and benefits for society at large, as well as a variety of financial and other benefits for the individuals who increase their educational attainment. We do not know what such policies and programs would cost. But the benefits to taxpayers appear to be sufficiently large that it is highly likely that they will exceed the costs and, consequently, yield positive net benefits to taxpayers. In sum, the likelihood that policies and programs that lead to increases in education will yield positive net benefits to taxpayers warrant extensive investigation into identifying and developing effective programs.

APPENDIX A
Data and Sources

Data

The SIPP contains 79,500 individuals with at least one monthly response in 2002. We excluded about 20,700 respondents who were not in the monthly sample for all 12 months and, consequently, did not provide data on full annual participation in social programs. We also excluded about 15,700 individuals who were under age 18. Finally, we excluded about 2,700 individuals who did not respond to the interview modules for immigration and medical participation. The result is a sample of 40,300 adults with annual income and participation data for 2002. We did not censure data in terms of age on the high end; the highest age in the final sample happens to be 86.

Unit of Analysis

The unit of analysis of this study is the individual. However, income taxes are based on family income, and some social support programs—welfare or food stamps, for example—target the family, not the individual. In estimating federal and state income taxes and benefits from family-oriented social support programs, we assume that income is evenly distributed among all adults in the particular household.

Educational Attainment

The key independent variable of the study is constructed from SIPP data. The related SIPP question asks for the highest degree received or grade completed, with 18 possible response choices. We mapped those choices into the four educational attainment categories used in this study. In situations where the response of a person to the education question varies along the year, June data dominates.

We performed similar mappings for surveys of the criminal justice system.

Population Identifiers

Because the effects of increased educational attainment may vary across population groups, we conducted separate analyses for each of eight population groups distinguished by gender and race/ethnicity (four groups). Some of the analyses also take account of an individual's age. The identifiers are routinely contained in all surveys used in this research. Depending on the case, the type of response might differ, such as one survey asking for age as of last birthday and another asking for birth date. Necessary mappings have been made whenever necessary.

"White" means that the individual has not declared any other race or ethnicity. "Black" means that the individual is a non-Hispanic black. "Asian" means a non-Hispanic, non-black Asian. Hispanic means that the individual is coded as a Hispanic. Necessary mappings have been made whenever necessary to convert survey responses to desired variable structure.

Taxation Data

For payroll taxes, we retrieved statutory taxation rates and the ceiling applicable to Medicare tax from the *Annual Statistical Supplement to the Social Security Bulletin, 2002* (Social Security Administration, 2002). For federal taxes, we obtained average 2002 taxation rates by income group from the Internal Revenue Service's *Statistics of Income Bulletin* (Parisi, 2004–2005). For state and local taxes, we sourced U.S. average taxation rates by income group from McIntyre et al. (2003).

The analysis uses these rates and applies them to earnings (payroll taxes) or personal or family income (for income taxes) from the SIPP (U.S. Census Bureau, 2005a, 2005b, 2005c).

Social Program Data

Program Participation

The SIPP provides participation data for all social support and insurance programs analyzed in this research. Basically, we use the survey's flag-type questions related to the respondent's participation in various programs. We assign participation the value of 1 if the response is positive for at least one month during 2002. For Medicare and Medicaid, we also make a distinction between outpatient and inpatient participation, since the benefit level varies tremendously between these two. Here, we interpret any participation as outpatient participation and hospitalization as inpatient participation.

Program Benefits

The SIPP provides a monthly benefit amount for welfare, food stamps, Unemployment Insurance, SSI, and Social Security. For such programs, the benefit is equal to the total across all months of 2002. For Medicare and Medicaid, we use data from the 2004 Medicare and Medicaid Statistical Supplement, published by the Centers for Medicare and Medicaid Services to compute average outpatient and inpatient benefit, based on total payments and number of beneficiaries in 2002. For subsidized housing, we use HUD data on 2002 program cost for public housing and Section 8 vouchers and number of residents covered to compute average housing subsidy per participant. We assume that unit housing cost per person is constant across education levels and demographic groups.

Incarceration Data

Participation

For state prisons, we use the 1997 Survey of Inmates in State and Federal Correctional Facilities, with a sample size of 18,000, to estimate the incarcerated population for each combination of education, age, race/ethnicity, gender, and place of birth. For each such combination, we weight the particular subsample by the corresponding sampling weight to estimate the national inmate population for that combination.

We follow the same procedure for county and municipal jails, using the 2002 Survey of Inmates of Local Jails. This survey has a sample size of 6,000. While this may seem small relative to the sample size of the Survey of Inmates in State and Federal Correctional Facilities, it is fairly adequate considering that the jail population totals about half of the state-prison population (665,000 versus 1.2 million in 2002).

Incarceration Costs

We use the *Sourcebook of Criminal Justice Statistics, 2003* (Pastore and Maguire, 2005) for computing per-inmate costs of incarceration in 2002. We use direct spending on state prisons and county and municipal jails, along with the number of inmates in state prisons and jails, to compute annual incarceration cost per inmate. Like we do with housing programs above, we assume that cost per inmate is the same regardless of the inmate's education level.

Cost of Education Data

To facilitate the analysis of the cost of post-elementary educational services, we aggregated grades into two education levels: high school and college.

The National Center for Education Statistics collects expenditure and attendance data from school districts and postsecondary education institutions to compute current expenditures per pupil. Expenditures per pupil are available on a per-ADA basis for K–12 school districts and on a per-FTE basis for postsecondary institutions. For this study, we used expenditure data for K–12 education for the 2001–2002 school year, the year closest to the calendar year, 2002, in which the SIPP data were collected. We used expenditure data for higher education for the 2000–2001 school year, the most recent available. All the expenditure data used in this study were obtained from the *Digest of Education Statistics: 2007* (U.S. Department of Education, National Center for Education Statistics, 2008).

APPENDIX B
Estimating Tax Payments

Payroll Taxes

The Social Security and hospital insurance portion of Medicare are financed by taxes levied on individual earnings. Not every individual pays these taxes; only the employed pay. Therefore, estimations are made using a two-part model. The first step estimates with probit the likelihood of paying payroll tax, and the second step estimates with OLS the amount of payroll tax payment conditional on having positive earnings. Assumed payroll tax payment for every individual is calculated by applying the statutory payroll tax rates (Table 3.3) to individual earnings data in SIPP. The specific response variable in the OLS is the square root of assumed payroll tax payments for an approximately normal distribution.

The independent variables are

- a set of dummies indicating the level of educational attainment:
  - less than high school graduate
  - some college
  - bachelor's degree or more
- age and age-squared
- interactions between educational attainment variables and age variables
- a set of race/ethnicity dummies for Asians, blacks, Hispanics, and Native Americans
- a dummy for U.S.-born versus immigrant.

Age is included as quadratic to allow for nonlinear effects of age, particularly as relates to cumulative experience in the labor market. Further, age and education status are interacted to allow for the slope on educational attainment to vary with age.

In all regressions, the intercept refers to the reference case of U.S.-born, white individuals who graduated from high school.

We run separate models for men and women, consistent with human-capital models of labor market outcomes. The fact that there are only small subsamples prevents us from running models for groups based on race/ethnicity and place of birth.

Depending on the nature of the social program in question, we run separate models for the elderly and non-elderly.

Estimation results are presented in Table B.1.

Table B.1
Estimates from Two-Part Model of 2002 Payroll Tax Payments

	Probit – Participation		OLS – Taxes Paid	
	Women	Men	Women	Men
Intercept	−0.8459**	−0.4249*	−4.1963	−4.15212
Education level				
Less than high school graduate	0.0891	−0.8238**	4.7728	2.2691
Some college	0.2686	−0.3459	−5.3807	−25.5432**
Bachelor's degree or more	0.2888	0.2851	−2.0267	1.0287
Age				
Age	0.1025**	0.1107**	2.5859**	3.2834**
Age squared	−0.0014**	−0.0016**	−0.0281**	−0.0357**
Age–less than high school graduate	−0.0307**	0.0110	−0.6790**	−0.5102*
Age–some college	−0.0036	0.0221	0.4990**	1.4644**
Age–bachelor's degree or more	−0.0049	0.0143	1.1552**	0.9948**
Age squared–less than high school graduate	0.0004**	0.0000	0.0079**	0.0058*
Age squared–some college	0.0000	−0.0002	−0.0051*	−0.0161**
Age squared–bachelor's degree or more	0.0001	−0.0002	−0.0143**	−0.0117**
Race/ethnicity				
Asian	−0.0745	−0.4392**	2.6975*	−2.7183*
Black	0.0284	−0.3238**	−1.2134*	−8.4983**
Hispanic	0.0334	0.0291	−0.7659	−4.1378**
Native American	0.0380	−0.2882*	−2.2908	−7.0643**
Immigrant	−0.1647**	0.2372**	−2.2035**	−0.4896
N	21,548	18,746	13,715	14,446
R squared	27%	35%	25%	31%

NOTES: One and two asterisks indicate significance at the 0.05 and 0.01 level, respectively. Education effects (main and interacted) are jointly significant in both models at the 0.0001 level. The intercept is high school graduate, white, U.S.-born.

Federal Income Taxes

While payroll taxes are paid by individuals, federal income taxes are paid by families (consisting of one or more individual) out of family income. Therefore, federal tax-payment estimations consist of a single regression of assumed per-person federal tax payment on educational attainment, age, and covariates. We calculate assumed federal tax payments by applying average federal income tax rates by income group (Table 3.2) to pre-transfer family income in the SIPP. This assumed federal tax payment for the family is divided by the number of adults in the family and logged (for normal distribution) to get the response variable for the OLS regression.

State and Local Taxes

State and local taxes are estimated like federal income taxes. We assume that such taxes are also paid out of total family income. Hence, state tax payment estimations also consist of a single regression. We calculate assumed state and local tax payments by applying national average U.S. rates (Table 3.4) to pre-transfer family income in the SIPP. Similar to federal taxes, state tax payments are also evenly divided among the adults in the household and logged for the OLS.

Table B.2 presents estimation results for amount of federal and state taxes.

Table B.2
Estimates of 2002 Federal and State Tax Payments

	Federal Taxes		State Taxes	
	OLS – Tax Paid (log)		OLS – Tax Paid (log)	
	Women	Men	Women	Men
Intercept	6.3700**	6.9522**	6.9718**	7.0804**
Education level				
Less than high school graduate	0.2453	−0.0928	0.1356	−0.0149
Some college	0.3375*	−0.0477	0.0993	−0.0509
Bachelor's degree or more	−0.0963	−0.2254	0.2832**	0.3602**
Age				
Age	0.0503**	0.0315**	0.0254**	0.0252**
Age squared	−0.0006**	−0.0004**	−0.0003**	−0.0003**
Age–less than high school graduate	−0.0378**	−0.0156*	−0.0208**	−0.0109**
Age–some college	0.0015	0.0157*	0.0049	0.0099**
Age–bachelor's degree or more	0.0417**	0.0459**	0.0110**	0.0070
Age squared–less than high school graduate	0.0004**	0.0001*	0.0002**	0.0001**
Age squared–some college	0.0000	−0.0002**	−0.0001*	−0.0001**
Age squared–bachelor's degree or more	−0.0004**	−0.0005**	−0.0001**	−0.0001*
Race/ethnicity				
Asian	0.0157	−0.1393**	−0.0575*	−0.1182**
Black	−0.5162**	−0.3944**	−0.2447**	−0.2116**
Hispanic	−0.2354**	−0.2686**	−0.1613**	−0.1882**
Native American	−0.4110**	−0.4564**	−0.2343**	−0.2694**
Immigrant	−0.0306	−0.1092**	−0.0572**	−0.0854**
N	21,400	18,644	21,352	18,614
R squared	26%	23%	27%	25%

NOTES: One and two asterisks indicate significance at the 0.05 and 0.01 levels, respectively. Education effects (main and interacted) are jointly significant in all models at the 0.0001 level. The intercept is high school graduate, white, U.S.-born.

APPENDIX C
Social Program Participation and Costs

Analytic Approach

In the standard income-leisure model, individuals trade off leisure and income. Under the presence of some guaranteed (but low) amount of income from social support and insurance programs, the particular outcome for any individual depends on his or her personal characteristics (preferences) and the wages that he or she can command in the labor market. The decision to participate in a social program is dictated by a comparison of the benefits available from that program and the earnings forgone in the labor market.

The more educated the individual, the more he or she can command in the labor market. Therefore, increased educational attainment makes leisure and program participation less attractive. Similarly, education can change an individual's preference curve, lowering the stigma for program utilization, thus moving him or her to a lower leisure point even assuming no change in wages. Usually, both wage and preference effects will act together to produce notable changes in behavior.

Therefore, we model program utilization and benefits as a function of income and individual attributes, including educational attainment. However, education also affects wages; i.e., it affects program use both directly and indirectly. We further reduce the model into one with two major inputs—education and other personal characteristics—as follows:

$$Y = f(E, D),$$

where Y is amount of program income, E is a measure of educational attainment, and D is a vector of demographic characteristics.

Program Utilization and Benefits Model

We divide the expected value of benefits received from a social program into two parts: (1) the probability of utilizing a program, i.e., receiving social support income, and (2) the expected amount of the benefit, conditional on utilization of the program.

For any given program, whether or not a person benefits from it is a dichotomous outcome and needs to be estimated separately from the benefit itself. Estimating the benefit on the entire population would yield erroneous estimates, since a lot of nonparticipating individuals would bias the picture. How the benefit level varies with personal attributes can only be assessed by analyzing those who receive any benefit.

For each program, the first part of the model is the individual's likelihood of program utilization as a function of education level and other demographics. The second part of the model is annual income from the program, conditional on positive program income, again as a function of education level and other characteristics.

We estimate the model in two parts. The first part consists of a probit regression in which the response variable equals 1 in the case of program utilization in 2002 and 0 otherwise. The second part of the estimation is an OLS regression in which the response variable is the respective program benefit of (or tax paid by) the individual in 2002. As incomes and, consequently, program benefits are not distributed normally, the second part of the model is typically run on transformed data (logarithmic).

The independent variables are as follows:

- a set of dummies indicating the level of educational attainment:
  - less than high school graduate
  - some college
  - bachelor's degree or more
- age and age-squared
- interactions between educational attainment variables and age variables
- a set of race/ethnicity dummies for Asians, blacks, Hispanics, and Native Americans
- a dummy for U.S.-born versus resident status.

Age is included as quadratic to allow for nonlinear effects of age, particularly as relates to cumulative experience in the labor market. Further, age and education status are interacted to allow for the slope on educational attainment to vary with age.

In all regressions, the intercept refers to the reference case of U.S.-born, white individuals who graduated from high school.

We run separate models for men and women, consistent with human-capital models of labor market outcomes. The fact that there are only small subsamples prevents us from running models for groups based on race/ethnicity and place of birth. Depending on the nature of the social program in question, we run separate models for the elderly and non-elderly.

Empirical Estimations

As explained before, our default strategy for estimating social program income consists of a program utilization part and a program income part that is conditional on utilization. We have used this approach to the fullest extent possible, including with those programs for which survey data includes not only participation but also program income data. For others, we use the utilization part of the model and apply it to average per-person program income estimated using administrative data.

In programs for which the data showed us a different participation or income pattern for the elderly as opposed to the non-elderly, we ran different regressions for the two age categories.

In a similar vein, for Medicare and Medicaid we used a two-part extension of the two-part model, since participation can be of two types—inpatient and outpatient—with substantially different benefit levels.

Welfare Programs

We gathered program income from Temporary Assistance to Needy Families, general assistance programs, and other welfare programs into a single "welfare program" figure since participation in any of the constituent programs was relatively low and the income amounts were small. Utilization of welfare means that the individual has utilized at least one of these three programs, and welfare income is the total the individual received across all three types of programs. The first part of the model estimates the likelihood of welfare utilization with probit, and the second part estimates the amount of welfare income conditional on utilization with OLS. The response variable in the income regression is the square root of total welfare income for normality. Results are presented in Table C.1.

Housing Programs

The subsidized housing programs analyzed in this study include the Public Housing program and the Section 8 Rental Voucher program, for which participation data are available in the SIPP. We estimate income from subsidized housing programs using the first part of the two-part model and applying its result to per-person average housing subsidy calculated from HUD data. The regression estimates the likelihood of receiving a housing subsidy (participation in at least one of the two programs) with probit. Utilization estimates are presented in Table C.2.

Table C.1
Estimated Two-Part Model of 2002 Welfare Income (Temporary Assistance to Needy Families, General Assistance, Other)

	Probit – Utilization		OLS – Income Received (square root)	
	Women	Men	Women	Men
Intercept	–1.8058**	–2.6872**	18.8502	33.5123
Education level				
Less than high school graduate	0.6111	–1.3400	–1.1258	–19.7075
Some college	–0.4260	–1.1202	29.3317	–28.3472
Bachelor's degree or more	–1.6583*	–0.7890	–57.1518	–38.3827
Age				
Age	0.0003	–0.0018	1.2803**	0.3010
Age squared	–0.0002	0.0000	–0.0173**	–0.0063
Age–less than high school graduate	0.0006	0.0681*	0.0988	0.6206
Age–some college	0.0084	0.0448	–1.4021	0.9710
Age–bachelor's degree or more	0.0304	0.0169	1.3635	1.3737
Age squared–less than high school graduate	–0.0001	–0.0007*	0.0009	–0.0055
Age squared–some college	0.0000	–0.0004	0.0154	–0.0103
Age squared–bachelor's degree or more	–0.0001	–0.0001	–0.0052	–0.0120
Race/ethnicity				
Asian	0.3010**	0.3124	17.3731**	12.7796
Black	0.5857**	0.4413**	3.2781	9.0014
Hispanic	0.3038**	0.1999	4.5635	5.5364
Native American	0.7274**	0.4846*	7.2424	10.1152
Immigrant	–0.1060	–0.0753	3.4162	6.4218
N	21,548	18,746	575	103
R squared	14%	5%	12%	22%

NOTES: One and two asterisks indicate significance at the 0.05 and 0.01 levels, respectively. Education effects (main and interacted) are jointly significant at the 0.05 level except for the income of men. The intercept is high school graduate, white, U.S.-born.

Table C.2
Estimates of 2002 Subsidized Housing Participation

	Probit – Utilization	
	Women	Men
Intercept	−0.71826**	−1.10238**
Education level		
Less than high school graduate	−0.29584	−0.10450
Some college	−0.32825	−0.57558
Bachelor's degree or more	−1.05488*	−0.78941
Age		
Age	−0.04159**	−0.03829**
Age squared	0.00036**	0.00035**
Age–less than high school graduate	0.02794**	0.01852
Age–some college	0.00686	0.02045
Age–bachelor's degree or more	0.02016	0.02895
Age squared–less than high school graduate	−0.00024*	−0.00018
Age squared–some college	−0.00003	−0.00021
Age squared–bachelor's degree or more	−0.00016	−0.00041
Race/ethnicity		
Asian	0.30835**	0.37206**
Black	0.80593**	0.58252**
Hispanic	0.33974**	0.36652**
Native American	0.47491**	0.66658**
Immigrant	−0.00510	0.13814*
N	21,548	18,746
R squared	11%	9%

NOTES: One and two asterisks indicate significance at the 0.05 and 0.01 levels, respectively. Education effects (main and interacted) are jointly significant at the 0.0001 level. The intercept is high school graduate, white, U.S.-born.

Food Stamps

Income from the Supplemental Nutrition Assistance Program is estimated using the two-part model. The first part of the model estimates the likelihood of food stamp utilization with probit, and the second part estimates the amount of food stamps received in the year conditional on utilization with OLS. The response variable in the income regression is the square root of food stamps income for normality. Results are presented in Table C.3.

Supplemental Security Income

We estimate income from the SSI program using the two-part model. The first part of the model estimates the likelihood of SSI utilization with probit, and the second part estimates the amount of SSI income received in the year conditional on utilization with OLS. The response variable in the income regression is the square root of SSI income for normality.

Further, as the SSI program comprises a supplemental subprogram for the elderly and a disability subprogram, we modeled program utilization and income separately for the elderly and non-elderly. Results are presented in Table C.4a for utilization and C.4b for income.

Table C.3
Estimated Two-Part Model of 2002 Food Stamp Income

	Probit – Utilization		OLS – Income Received (square root)	
	Women	Men	Women	Men
Intercept	−1.0766**	−2.4361**	41.0327**	0.8122
Education level				
Less than high school graduate	0.3603	−0.3407	5.7363	31.4441**
Some college	−1.0525**	−0.4754	−1.1340	7.7287
Bachelor's degree or more	−0.7235	0.0402	2.5046	53.1373
Age				
Age	−0.0061	0.0336**	0.1033	1.2532**
Age squared	−0.0001	−0.0005**	−0.0058**	−0.0148**
Age–less than high school graduate	0.0044	0.0231	−0.2122	−1.3383**
Age–some college	0.0318*	0.0059	0.0116	−0.3870
Age–bachelor's degree or more	−0.0230	−0.0359	−0.6522	−2.4458*
Age squared–less than high school graduate	0.0000	−0.0001	0.0023	0.0136**
Age squared–some college	−0.0003	0.0000	−0.0001	0.0045
Age squared–bachelor's degree or more	0.0004	0.0005	0.0090	0.0260*
Race/ethnicity				
Asian	0.0721	0.1240	6.4447*	6.7825
Black	0.7664**	0.3937**	3.6310**	4.3408*
Hispanic	0.2852**	0.0762	1.7749	1.7159
Native American	0.6623**	0.5553**	7.9107**	5.1160
Immigrant	−0.1211*	−0.1347	−0.3359	3.4727
N	21,547	18,746	1,720	521
R squared	17%	8%	20%	7%

NOTES: One and two asterisks indicate significance at the 0.05 and 0.01 levels, respectively. Education effects (main and interacted) are jointly significant at the 0.0001 level except for income of men. The intercept is high school graduate, white, U.S.-born.

Table C.4a
Estimated Two-Part Model of 2002 SSI Income

	Probit – Utilization			
	Women		Men	
	Under 65	Over 64	Under 65	Over 64
Intercept	–2.0268**	–27.8359*	–1.9367**	25.8037
Education level				
Less than high school graduate	–0.4308	32.9250*	–0.2124	–30.2471
Some college	–1.7121**	33.9746	–0.5300	–40.3907
Bachelor's degree or more	–2.5918	28.2667	–1.5317	–23.9030
Age				
Age	0.0011	0.6581*	–0.0053	–0.7630
Age squared	0.0001	–0.0042*	0.0001	0.0051
Age–less than high school graduate	0.0413	–0.8362*	0.0377	0.8564
Age–some college	0.0631*	–0.8761	0.0022	1.0533
Age–bachelor's degree or more	0.0766	–0.7675	0.0192	0.6412
Age squared–less than high school graduate	–0.0003	0.0054*	–0.0005	–0.0059
Age squared–some college	–0.0006	0.0056	0.0001	–0.0068
Age squared–bachelor's degree or more	–0.0008	0.0051	–0.0001	–0.0043
Race/ethnicity				
Asian	0.3310**	0.8373**	0.3708**	1.0688**
Black	0.4435**	0.9025**	0.4652**	0.7945**
Hispanic	–0.0244	1.0538**	0.1406	0.7823**
Native American	0.2809	0.6950	0.1994	1.3208**
Immigrant	–0.4631**	0.4073**	–0.2948**	0.5750**
N	17,435	4,111	15,813	2,927
R squared	15%	22%	11%	25%

NOTES: One and two asterisks indicate significance at the 0.05 and 0.01 levels, respectively. Education effects (main and interacted) are jointly significant in all models at the 0.0001 level. The intercept is high school graduate, white, U.S.-born.

Table C.4b
Estimated Two-Part Model of 2002 SSI Income

	OLS - Income Received (square root)			
	Women		Men	
	Under 65	Over 64	Under 65	Over 64
Intercept	50.373**	−225.989	54.661**	663.241
Education level				
Less than high school graduate	−8.084	588.206	−3.095	−408.058
Some college	−35.041	282.255	−57.511	−497.993
Bachelor's degree or more	−10.853	728.839	47.046	−1076.274
Age				
Age	0.615	7.238	0.420	−14.173
Age squared	−0.007	−0.049	−0.003	0.079
Age–less than high school graduate	0.718	−15.785	0.356	9.019
Age–some college	1.395	−6.525	2.941	13.755
Age–bachelor's degree or more	−1.078	−18.354	−2.890	26.134
Age squared–less than high school graduate	−0.011	0.106	−0.006	−0.049
Age squared–some college	−0.015	0.037	−0.036	−0.094
Age squared–bachelor's degree or more	0.021	0.116	0.033	−0.158
Race/ethnicity				
Asian	−3.835	17.298**	1.190	31.636**
Black	−2.118	1.792	−1.527	−3.764
Hispanic	1.438	2.942	−2.193	5.874
Native American	11.138*	−22.053**	5.213	−13.803
Immigrant	−1.279	9.889**	−0.490	−5.013
N	687	316	452	138
R squared	5%	14%	3%	24%

NOTES: One and two asterisks indicate significance at the 0.05 and 0.01 levels, respectively. Education effects (main and interacted) are jointly significant for under-65 women at the 0.005 level. The intercept is high school graduate, white, U.S.-born.

Medicaid

The SIPP does not report Medicaid payments on behalf of a respondent. For each respondent, it reports whether the respondent was covered by Medicaid, the number of medical provider visits in the previous 12 months, and whether the respondent was hospitalized in the previous 12 months. We use a two-part model to estimate benefits from the Medicaid program. The first part estimates Medicaid utilization, the probability that a respondent covered by Medicaid had at least one medical provider visit in the previous 12 months. The second part estimates hospitalization, conditional on Medicaid utilization. We assume that Medicaid utilization absent hospitalization is outpatient utilization. We assume that hospitalization is inpatient utilization.

As the SIPP provides utilization but not benefit data, we compute per-person average inpatient as well as outpatient benefits from Centers for Medicare and Medicaid Services data.

As our analysis of the age profile of Medicaid participants and nonparticipants did not indicate anything remotely resembling a transition point based on age, we did not separately model Medicaid utilization for the elderly and non-elderly. Estimates are presented in Table C.5.

Medicare

The SIPP does not report Medicare payments on behalf of a respondent. For each respondent, it reports whether the respondent was covered by Medicare, the number of medical provider visits in the previous 12 months, and whether the respondent was hospitalized in the previous 12 months. We use a two-part model to estimate benefits from the Medicare program. The first part estimates Medicare utilization, the probability that a respondent covered by Medicare had at least one medical provider visit in the previous 12 months. The second part estimates hospitalization, conditional on Medicare utilization. We assume that Medicare utilization absent hospitalization is outpatient utilization. We assume that hospitalization is inpatient utilization.

As the SIPP provides utilization but not benefit data, we compute per-person average inpatient as well as outpatient benefits from CMS data.

As Medicare is primarily a health care insurance program for the elderly but also a disability and renal-disease program regardless of age, we modeled Medicare utilization separately for the elderly and non-elderly. An analysis of the age distribution of participants and nonparticipants also supports this choice for mere utilization (not hospitalization). Estimates are presented in Table C.6.

Table C.5
Estimates of 2002 Medicaid Participation

	Probit – Utilization		Probit – Hospitalization	
	Women	Men	Women	Men
Intercept	0.2995*	–1.0325**	–0.7821**	–2.7053**
Education level				
Less than high school graduate	–0.3366	0.1364	0.1549	0.6601
Some college	–0.9617**	–0.2695	–0.1318	1.7033*
Bachelor's degree or more	–1.4920**	–1.5242**	–2.5823*	0.9136
Age				
Age	–0.0598**	–0.0214**	–0.0010	0.0646**
Age squared	0.0005**	0.0002**	0.0000	–0.0005*
Age–less than high school graduate	0.0393**	0.0159	–0.0111	–0.0240
Age–some college	0.0254**	–0.0038	0.0032	–0.0729*
Age–bachelor's degree or more	0.0176	0.0244	0.1142*	–0.0393
Age squared–less than high school graduate	–0.0004**	–0.0002	0.0002	0.0003
Age squared–some college	–0.0002*	0.0001	0.0000	0.0007*
Age squared–bachelor's degree or more	0.0000	–0.0001	–0.0011*	0.0004
Race/ethnicity				
Asian	0.3955**	0.5279**	–0.5340**	–0.2137
Black	0.6226**	0.5057**	–0.1194	–0.0524
Hispanic	0.3447**	0.2433**	–0.0620	–0.1925
Native American	0.9122**	1.0390**	–0.3817*	–0.0795
Immigrant	–0.0502	0.0116**	–0.1414	–0.0883
N	21,548	18,746	3,181	1,596
R squared	14%	11%	2%	5%

NOTES: One and two asterisks indicate significance at the 0.05 and 0.01 levels, respectively. Education effects (main and interacted) are jointly significant at the 0.05 level except for women's hospitalization. The intercept is high school graduate, white, U.S.-born.

Table C.6
Estimates of 2002 Medicare Participation

	Probit – Utilization				Probit – Hospitalization	
	Women		Men			
	Under 65	Over 64	Under 65	Over 64	Women	Men
Intercept	−0.7227**	−9.8709	−0.7444*	−18.1862	0.4278	−1.2382
Education level						
Less than high school graduate	−0.3954	−5.3939	−1.2145**	12.4510	−1.1342	0.0410
Some college	−1.3210**	2.1560	−0.4884	14.8332	1.7160	4.4829**
Bachelor's degree or more	0.1055	−9.1268	3.0736**	20.0691	3.5643	4.4922*
Age						
Age	−0.1040**	0.3076	−0.1040**	0.4964	−0.0480*	0.0052
Age squared	0.0017**	−0.0019	0.0017**	−0.0030	0.0004*	0.0000
Age–less than high school graduate	0.0315	0.1322	0.0909**	−0.3035	0.0344	−0.0011
Age–some college	0.0538*	−0.0652	0.0155	−0.3758	−0.0527	−0.1457**
Age–bachelor's degree or more	−0.0251	0.2132	−0.1693**	−0.5134	−0.0946	−0.1451*
Age squared–less than high school graduate	−0.0003	−0.0008	−0.0011**	0.0018	−0.0002	0.0000
Age squared–some college	−0.0006	0.0005	−0.0001	0.0023	0.0004	0.0011**
Age squared–bachelor's degree or more	0.0002	−0.0013	0.0018**	0.0032	0.0006	0.0011*
Race/ethnicitiy						
Asian	−0.0354	−0.8993**	0.1210	−0.8180**	−0.1793	−0.1541
Black	0.2663*	−0.5305**	0.2684**	−0.3562*	0.1127	0.0222
Hispanic	−0.1181	−0.6390**	0.0085	−0.4498*	−0.0794	−0.0327
Native American	−0.2333	n/a	−0.0400	−0.5629	−0.4789	0.5325
Immigrant	−0.3839**	−0.6440**	−0.3543**	−0.5973**	−0.0818	−0.0279
N	17,437	4,300	15,819	3,109	4,760	3,550
R squared	24%	17%	23%	11%	1%	2%

NOTES: One and two asterisks indicate significance at the 0.05 and 0.01 levels, respectively. Education effects (main and interacted) are jointly significant in all models at the 0.05 level or better. The intercept is high school graduate, white, U.S.-born. Native American dropped in one model since it predicts participation perfectly.

Unemployment Insurance

We estimate income from the Unemployment Insurance program using the two-part model. The first part of the model estimates the likelihood of utilizing Unemployment Insurance with probit, and the second part estimates the amount of unemployment compensation received in the year conditional on utilization with OLS. The response variable in the income regression is logged compensation for normality. Results are presented in Table C.7.

Social Security

We estimate income from the Social Security program using a two-part model. The first part of the model estimates the likelihood of Social Security utilization with probit, and the second part estimates the amount of Social Security income received in the year conditional on utilization with OLS. The response variable in the income regression is the square root of Social Security income for normality.

Further, like SSI, the Social Security program includes a retirement benefits sub-program that can kick in starting age 62, and survivor and disability insurance programs that might be applicable regardless of age. Therefore, we modeled program utilization and income separately for the elderly and non-elderly, using 62 as the transition age (the actual age profile of users in the SIPP confirms this). Results are presented in Table C.8a for utilization and C.8b for income.

Table C.7
Estimated Two-Part Model of 2002 Unemployment Insurance Income

	Probit – Utilization		OLS – Income Received (log)	
	Women	Men	Women	Men
Intercept	–2.9330**	–2.7915**	6.5966**	5.4985**
Education level				
Less than high school graduate	–1.0009*	–0.6468	–0.0920	0.6086
Some college	–0.3783	0.3015	–2.8881	–0.7770
Bachelor's degree or more	0.0558	0.1622	0.3156	–0.0034
Age				
Age	0.0689**	0.0736**	0.0434	0.0938*
Age squared	–0.0009**	–0.0009**	–0.0005	–0.0009
Age–less than high school graduate	0.0506*	0.0236	–0.0135	–0.0340
Age–some college	0.0213	–0.0220	0.1267	0.0408
Age–bachelor's degree or more	–0.0074	–0.0214	0.0013	0.0191
Age squared–less than high school graduate	–0.0006*	–0.0002	0.0003	0.0003
Age squared–some college	–0.0003	0.0003	–0.0012	–0.0005
Age squared–bachelor's degree or more	0.0000	0.0003	0.0000	–0.0003
Race/ethnicity				
Asian	0.2155*	–0.3135**	–0.0871	–0.1421
Black	0.0366	–0.1172	–0.0522	–0.4183**
Hispanic	0.0561	–0.0118	–0.2305	–0.0820
Native American	–0.0264	0.1424	–0.5235	–0.6706**
Immigrant	–0.0996	–0.0452	0.1750	–0.0767
N	21,546	18,743	731	846
R squared	5%	4%	9%	10%

NOTES: One and two asterisks indicate significance at the 0.05 and 0.01 levels, respectively. Education effects (main and interacted) are jointly significant at the 0.001 level except for income of men. The intercept is high school graduate, white, U.S.-born.

Table C.8a
Estimated Two-Part Model of 2002 Social Security Income

	Probit – Utilization			
	Women		Men	
	Under 63	Over 62	Under 63	Over 62
Intercept	−0.8709**	−38.3540**	0.0168	−39.7909**
Education level				
Less than high school graduate	0.6073	11.6547	−1.0941*	−3.3403
Some college	−0.2531	−8.8868	−1.7712**	−0.9760
Bachelor's degree or more	0.4972	−2.1232	0.8328	−2.8323
Age				
Age	−0.0797**	1.0465**	−0.1260**	1.0692**
Age squared	0.0014**	−0.0067**	0.0019**	−0.0068**
Age–less than high school graduate	−0.0195	−0.3054	0.0818**	0.1079
Age–some college	−0.0068	0.2453	0.0706**	0.0452
Age–bachelor's degree or more	−0.0627	0.0413	−0.0668	0.0865
Age squared–less than high school graduate	0.0003	0.0020	−0.0010**	−0.0009
Age squared–some college	0.0002	−0.0017	−0.0007*	−0.0004
Age squared–Bachelor's degree or more	0.0008	−0.0002	0.0008	−0.0007
Race/ethnicity				
Asian	−0.2945*	−0.8425**	−0.0287	−0.7392**
Black	0.1991**	−0.4224**	0.2511**	−0.2427*
Hispanic	−0.1717*	−0.5322**	−0.0883	−0.1703
Native American	−0.1402	0.4043	0.0629	−0.5236
Immigrant	−0.2676**	−0.4689**	−0.2834**	−0.5085**
N	16,969	4,782	15,391	3,526
R squared	20%	19%	16%	19%

NOTES: One and two asterisks indicate significance at the 0.05 and 0.01 levels, respectively. Education effects (main and interacted) are jointly significant in all models at the 0.01 level. The intercept is high school graduate, white, U.S.-born.

Table C.8b
Estimated Two-Part Model of 2002 Social Security Income

	OLS - Income Received (square root)			
	Women		Men	
	Under 63	Over 62	Under 63	Over 62
Intercept	46.992**	203.691**	5.060	117.329
Education level				
Less than high school graduate	1.545	−200.299*	54.423**	182.044
Some college	−38.776	−147.853	21.444	−81.622
Bachelor's degree or more	116.283	−2.247	160.677*	−329.631*
Age				
Age	0.636	−3.662*	2.754**	−0.291
Age squared	−0.004	0.028*	−0.021*	0.001
Age–less than high school graduate	−0.358	5.198*	−2.783*	−5.361
Age–some college	1.801	4.034	−0.619	2.109
Age–bachelor's degree or more	−3.289	0.240	−7.069*	8.858*
Age squared–less than high school graduate	0.005	−0.034*	0.029*	0.038
Age squared–some college	−0.019	−0.027	0.002	−0.013
Age squared–bachelor's degree or more	0.023	−0.002	0.070	−0.058*
Race/ethnicity				
Asian	−3.966	−7.041*	1.663	−13.146**
Black	−0.050	−4.222**	−5.740*	−8.923**
Hispanic	−3.774	−7.250**	0.951	−7.775**
Native American	−14.760*	−2.995	2.303	−10.555
Immigrant	−4.545	−2.519	−7.490	−4.066*
N	1,039	4,418	764	3,203
R squared	5%	7%	16%	7%

NOTES: One and two asterisks indicate significance at the 0.05 and 0.01 levels, respectively. Education effects (main and interacted) are jointly significant in all models at the 0.01 level. The intercept is high school graduate, white, U.S.-born.

APPENDIX D
Incarceration Cost Estimations

Our approach to estimating incarceration spending is a variant of the two-part model. The first part estimates the likelihood of becoming an inmate and uses individual data from surveys of the criminal justice system and the general population. The second part uses administrative data to calculate per-person estimated incarceration spending, like some social support and insurance programs for which benefit data are not available in surveys.

Probability of Incarceration

Prisons

We estimate the probability of imprisonment at the individual level as the number of prisoners in each demographic category divided by the general population for that category. We use the 1997 administration of the Survey of Inmates in State and Federal Correctional Facilities to estimate the incarcerated population for each combination of education level, age, race/ethnicity, and gender. We use the 1997 Current Population Survey to estimate general population counts in each corresponding subgroup. Because the Current Population Survey does not include incarcerated persons, we calculate the probability of incarceration as the number of prisoners in each population category divided by the sum of the general population and the number of prisoners for that category. Per-person prison spending computed from the *Sourcebook of Criminal Justice 2003* (Pastore and Maguire, 2007), shown in Table 5.2, constitutes the second part of the two-part model.

Jails

We estimate the probability of being jailed at the individual level as the number of jail inmates in each demographic category divided by the general population for that category. We use the 2002 Survey of Inmates of Local Jails to estimate the jail population for each combination of education level, age, race/ethnicity, and gender. We use the 2002 Current Population Survey to estimate general population counts in each corresponding subgroup. Here, too, because the Current Population Survey does not include incarcerated persons, we calculate the probability of incarceration as the number of prisoners in each population category divided by the sum of the general population and the number of prisoners for that category. Like prisons, per-person jail spending computed from the *Sourcebook of Criminal Justice, 2003* (Pastore and Maguire, 2007), shown in Table 5.2, constitutes the second part of the two-part model.

As incarceration-probability estimations are not based on regressions, they consist of a sizeable matrix for prisons and jails each, with five dimensions (educational attainment, age, gender, race/ethnicity, and place of birth). Such output is not depicted here, but the data are available from the authors upon request.

References

Aos, Steve, Roxanne Lieb, Jim Mayfield, Marna Miller, and Annie Pennucci, *Benefits and Costs of Prevention and Early Intervention Programs for Youth*, Washington State Institute for Public Policy, Olympia, Wash., July 2004.

Arias, Elizabeth, "United States Life Tables, 2002," *National Vital Statistics Reports*, Vol. 53, No. 6, November 10, 2004.

Ashenfelter, Orley, Colm Harmon, and Hessel Oosterbeek, "A Review of Estimates of the Schooling/Earnings Relationship, with Tests for Publication Bias," *Labor Economics*, Vol. 6, No. 4, November 1999.

Beck, Allen J., and Bernard E. Shipley, *Recidivism of Prisoners Released in 1983*, Bureau of Justice Statistics Special Report, NCJ-116261, U.S. Department of Justice, 1989.

Becker, Gary S., "Human Capital and Poverty," *Religion and Liberty*, Vol. 8, No. 1, January–February 1998.

Bee, M. and P.J. Dolton, "Costs and Economies of Scale in U.K. Private Schools," *Applied Economics*, April 1985.

Belfield, Clive R., and Henry M. Levin, *The Economic Losses from High School Dropouts in California*, California Dropout Research Project Report #1, Santa Barbara, Calif.: University of California, Gevirtz Graduate School of Education, 2007.

Belfield, Clive R., Milagros Nores, Steve Barnett, and Lawrence Schweinhart, "The High/Scope Perry Preschool Program: Cost-Benefit Analysis Using Data from the Age-40 Followup," *Journal of Human Resources*, Vol. 41, No. 1, Winter 2006.

Benjamin, Roger, and Stephen Carroll, *Breaking the Social Contract: the Fiscal Crisis in Higher Education*, Santa Monica, Calif.: RAND Corporation, CAE-100, 1997.

Butler, R.J. and D.H. Monk, "The Cost of Public Schooling in New York State," *Journal of Human Resources*, Summer 1985.

Card, David, "The Causal Effect of Education on Earnings," in Orley Ashenfelter and David Card, eds., *Handbook of Labor Economics*, Vol. 3A, Amsterdam: Elsevier Science, 1999.

Carroll, Stephen J., Cathy Krop, Jeremy Arkes, Peter A. Morrison, and Ann Flanagan, *California's K–12 Public Schools: How Are They Doing?* Santa Monica, Calif.: RAND Corporation, MG-186-EDU, 2005. As of May 6, 2009:
http://www.rand.org/pubs/monographs/MG186/

Chakraborty, Kalyan, Basudeb Biswas, and W. Cris Lewis, "Economies of Scale in Public Education: An Econometric Analysis," *Contemporary Economic Policy*, Vol. 18, No. 2, April 2000.

Dee, Thomas S., "Are There Civic Benefits to Education?" *Journal of Public Economics*, Vol. 88, 2004.

Duan, Naihua, Willard G. Manning, Jr., Carl N. Morris, and Joseph P. Newhouse, "A Comparison of Alternative Models for the Demand for Medical Care," *Journal of Business and Economic Statistics*, Vol. 1, No. 2, 1983, pp. 115–126.

Ehrlich, Isaac, "On the Relation Between Education and Crime," in F. Thomas Juster, ed., *Education, Income, and Human Behavior*, New York: McGraw-Hill, 1975.

Freeman, Richard, "Why Do So Many Young American Men Commit Crimes and What Might We Do About It?" *Journal of Economic Perspectives*, Vol. 10, No. 1, Winter 1996.

Gage, Tim, and Matt Newman, *Cumulative Impact: How Cuts to Higher Education in the Recent Past, Today and in the Near Future Will Affect Access and Opportunity for California Students*, Sacramento, Calif.: The Campaign for College Opportunity, April 2008.

Garland, David, *Culture of Control: Crime and Social Order in Contemporary Society*, Chicago: University of Chicago Press, 2001.

Gilmore, Ruth Wilson, "Spend Cash on Schools, Not on Building Prisons," *Los Angeles Daily News*, June 30, 2005.

Hagan, John, and Ronit Dinovitzer, "Collateral Consequences of Imprisonment for Children, Communities, and Prisoners," in Michael Tonry and Joan Petersilia, eds., *Prisons*, Chicago: University of Chicago Press, 1999.

Harbison, Frederick, and Charles Myers, eds., *Manpower and Education*, New York: McGraw-Hill, 1965.

Harlow, Caroline Wolf, *Education and Correctional Populations*, Bureau of Justice Statistics Special Report, NCJ-195-670, U.S. Department of Justice, 2003.

Haveman, Robert H., and Barbara L. Wolfe, "Schooling and Economic Well-Being: The Role of Nonmarket Effects," *Journal of Human Resources*, Vol. 19, No. 3, 1984.

Johnson, Hans, and Deborah Reed, "Can California Import Enough College Graduates to Meet Workforce Needs?" *California Counts: Population Trends and Profiles*, Vol. 8, No. 4, Public Policy Institute of California, San Francisco, Calif., 2007.

Karoly, Lynn A., *Valuing Benefits in Benefit-Cost Studies of Social Programs*, Santa Monica, Calif.: RAND Corporation, TR-643-MCF, RAND, 2008. As of May 6, 2009:
http://www.rand.org/pubs/technical_reports/TR643/

Karoly, Lynn A., and James H. Bigelow, *The Economics of Investing in Universal Preschool Education in California*, Santa Monica, Calif.: RAND Corporation, 2005, MG-349-PF. As of May 6, 2009:
http://www.rand.org/pubs/monographs/MG349/

Kelly, Patrick J., *As America Becomes More Diverse: The Impact of State Higher Education Inequality*, Boulder, Colo.: National Center for Higher Education Management Systems, November 2005.

Krop, Cathy S., Stephen J. Carroll, and Randy L. Ross, *Tracking K–12 Education Spending in California*, Santa Monica, Calif.: RAND Corporation, MR-548-SFR, 1995. As of May 6, 2009:
http://www.rand.org/pubs/monograph_reports/MR548/

Krop, Richard, *The Social Returns to Increased Investment in Education: Measuring the Effect of Education on the Cost of Social Programs*, Santa Monica, Calif.: RAND Corporation, RGSD-138, 1998. As of May 6, 2009:
http://www.rand.org/pubs/rgs_dissertations/RGSD138/

Krop, Richard, Stephen J. Carroll, Georges Vernez, and C. Peter Rydell, *The Return to Increased Public Expenditures on Education*, Santa Monica, Calif.: RAND Corporation, DRU-2316-CAE, 2000. As of May 6, 2009:
http://www.rand.org/pubs/drafts/DRU2316/

Krueger, Alan B., and Mikael Lindahl, "Education for Growth: Why and for Whom?" *Journal of Economic Literature*, Vol. 39, December 2001.

Kumar, R.C., "Economies of Scale in School Operation: Evidence from Canada," *Applied Economics*, Vol. 15, No. 3, 1983.

Lochner, Lance, "Education, Work, and Crime: A Human Capital Approach," *International Economic Review*, Vol. 45, No. 3, August 2004.

Lochner, Lance, and Enrico Moretti, "The Effect of Education on Crime: Evidence from Prison Inmates, Arrests, And Self-Reports," *American Economic Review*, Vol. 94, No. 1, March 2004.

Machin, Stephen, and Costas Meghir, *Crime and Economic Incentives*, Institute for Fiscal Studies, Working Paper No. 00/17, 2000.

Masse, Leonard N., and W. Steven Barnett, *A Benefit Cost Analysis of the Abecedarian Early Childhood Intervention*, New Brunswick, N.J.: National Institute for Educational Research, 2002.

McIntyre, Robert, Robert Denk, Norton Francis, Matthew Gardner, Will Gomaa, Fiona Hsu, and Richard Sims, *Who Pays? A Distributional Analysis of the Tax Systems in All 50 States*, 2nd Edition, Washington, D.C.: Institute on Taxation and Economic Policy, 2003.

Mincer, Jacob, "Education and Unemployment," in Jacob Mincer, ed., *Studies of Human Capital*, Cambridge, UK: Edward Elgar, 1993.

Moffitt, Robert, "Incentive Effects of the U.S. Welfare System: A Review," *Journal of Economic Literature*, Vol. 30, No. 1, March 1992.

Parisi, Michael, "Individual Income Tax Rates and Shares, 2002," Internal Revenue Service *Statistics of Income Bulletin*, Winter 2004–2005. As of May 7, 2009:
http://www.irs.treas.gov/taxstats/bustaxstats/article/0,,id=137167,00.html

Pastore, Ann L., and Kathleen Maguire, eds., *Sourcebook of Criminal Justice Statistics, 2003*, Bureau of Justice Statistics Special Report, NCJ 208756, U.S. Department of Justice, 2005. As of May 7, 2009, more recent editions available at:
http://www.albany.edu/sourcebook/

Pettit, Becky, and Bruce Western, "Mass Imprisonment and the Life Course: Race and Class Inequality in U.S. Incarceration," *American Sociological Review*, Vol. 69, No. 2, April 2004.

Reynolds, Arthur J., Judy A. Temple, Dylan L. Robertson, and Emily A. Mann, "Age 21 Cost-Benefit Analysis of the Title I Chicago Child-Parent Centers," *Educational Evaluation and Policy Analysis*, Vol. 24, No. 4, Winter 2002.

Riew, John, "Scale Economies, Capacity Utilization, and School Costs: A Comparative Analysis of Secondary and Elementary Schools," *Journal of Education Finance*, Spring 1986.

Rouse, Cecilia, "The Labor Market Consequences of an Inadequate Education," presented at the Equity Symposium on "The Social Costs of Inadequate Education," Teachers' College, Columbia University, New York, September 2005.

Social Security Administration, Office of Policy, *Annual Statistical Supplement to the Social Security Bulletin, 2002*, Washington, D.C., December 2002. As of May 7, 2009:
http://www.ssa.gov/policy/docs/statcomps/supplement/2002/

———, *Annual Statistical Supplement to the Social Security Bulletin, 2003*, SSA Publication No. 13-11700, Washington, D.C., July 2004. As of May 7, 2009:
http://www.ssa.gov/policy/docs/statcomps/supplement/2003/

———, Program Highlights 2005, Web page. As of March 2006:
http://www.ssa.gov/policy/docs/quickfacts/prog_highlights/index.html

Stacey, Nevzer, "Social Benefits of Education," *Annals of the American Academy of Political and Social Science*, Vol. 559. No. 1, September 1998, pp. 54–63.

Steffensmeier, Darrell, and Stephen Demuth, "Ethnicity and Sentencing Outcomes in U.S. Federal Courts: Who Is Punished More Harshly?" *American Sociological Review*, Vol. 65, No. 5, October 2000.

Steinhauer, Jennifer, "Prisons Push California to Seek New Approach," *New York Times*, December 11, 2006.

Stephan, James J., *State Prison Expenditures 2001*, Bureau of Justice Statistics Special Report, NCJ 202949, U.S. Department of Justice, June 2004.

Uccello, Cori E., and L. Jerome Gallagher, *General Assistance Programs: The State-Based Part of the Safety Net*, Washington, D.C.: Urban Institute, January 1997.

U.S. Census Bureau, Survey of Income and Program Participation 2002 Panel, Waves 1–9 Core—Longitudinal Microdata File, Washington, D.C., 2005a. As of May 7, 2009:
http://www.census.gov/sipp/

———, Survey of Income and Program Participation 2002 Panel, Wave 2 Topical Module Microdata File, Washington, D.C., 2005b. As of May 7, 2009:
http://www.census.gov/sipp/

———, Survey of Income and Program Participation 2002 Panel, Wave 6 Topical Module Microdata File, Washington, D.C., 2005c. As of May 7, 2009:
http://www.census.gov/sipp/

U.S. Census Bureau and Bureau of Labor Statistics, Current Population Survey, various years. As of May 8, 2009:
http://www.census.gov/cps/

U.S. Department of Education, National Center for Education Statistics, *The Condition of Education 2006*, Washington, D.C., 2006. As of May 7, 2009:
http://nces.ed.gov/programs/coe/

———, *Digest of Education Statistics: 2007*, Washington, D.C., March 2008. As of May 7, 2009:
http://nces.ed.gov/programs/digest/d07

U.S. Department of Health and Human Services, Centers for Medicare and Medicaid Services, *Medicare and Medicaid Statistical Supplement, 2004*, 2006. Updated edition, as of May 7, 2009:
http://www.cms.hhs.gov/MedicareMedicaidStatSupp/

U.S. Department of Justice, Bureau of Justice Statistics, and U.S. Department of Justice, Federal Bureau of Prisons, Survey of Inmates in State and Federal Correctional Facilities, 1997 [Computer file]. Compiled by U.S. Department of Commerce, Bureau of the Census. ICPSR ed. Ann Arbor, MI: Inter-University Consortium for Political and Social Research, 2001. As of May 7, 2009:
http://www.icpsr.umich.edu/NACJD/sisfcf/

U.S. Department of Justice, Bureau of Justice Statistics, Survey of Inmates in Local Jails, 2002 [Computer file]. Conducted by U.S. Department of Commerce, Bureau of the Census. ICPSR04359-v2. Ann Arbor, MI: Inter-university Consortium for Political and Social Research, 2006. As of May 7, 2009:
http://www.icpsr.umich.edu/cocoon/NACJD/SERIES/00069.xml

Vernez, Georges, Richard A. Krop, C. Peter Rydell, *Closing the Education Gap: Benefits and Costs*, Santa Monica, Calif.: RAND Corporation, MR-1036-EDU, 1999. As of May 6, 2009:
http://www.rand.org/pubs/monograph_reports/MR1036/

Viscusi, W. Kip, "Market Incentives for Criminal Behavior," in Richard B. Freeman and Harry J. Holzer, eds., *The Black Youth Employment Crisis*, Chicago: University of Chicago Press, 1986.

Western, Bruce, Jeffrey R. Kling, and David F. Weiman, "The Labor Market Consequences of Incarceration," *Crime and Delinquency*, Vol. 47, No. 3, July 2001.

Wolfe, Barbara, and Samuel Zuvekas, "Nonmarket Outcomes of Schooling, Institute for Research and Poverty," Discussion Paper 1065-95, University of Wisconsin-Madison, May 1995.